A
MAN
AND HIS PAN

A
MAN
AND HIS PAN

JOHN BOSWELL
WITH SUSAN WYLER

Andrews McMeel
Publishing

Kansas City

Book design by Barbara Cohen Aronica
Cover design by Richard Rossiter
Cover photography by E.H. Wallop
Cover computer imaging by John Barrett
Illustrations by Ron Barrett

ISBN: 0-8382-7854-2

www.andrewsmcmeel.com

99 00 01 02 03 RDC 10 9 8 7 6 5 4 3 2 1

Library of Congress Cataloging-in-Publication Data on File

CONTENTS

INTRODUCTION vii

CHAPTER ONE
GREAT PAN BREAKFASTS:
MORE THAN JUST EGGS 1

CHAPTER TWO
STEAKS AND CHOPS:
THE MEAT OF THE MATTER 29

CHAPTER THREE
CHICKEN IN THE PAN 63

CHAPTER FOUR
SEAFOOD IN THE PAN 99

CHAPTER FIVE
ONE-PAN MEALS 123

CHAPTER SIX
THE SHORT-ORDER GOURMET 165

CHAPTER SEVEN
SIDES FOR ALL OCCASIONS 197

CHAPTER EIGHT
PAN COOKING FOR KIDS 229

INDEX 252

SMELL THE SIZZLE, EAT THE STEAK
Welcome to *A Man and His Pan*

I am so excited about some of the flavors and taste sensations that you are going to experience here, I wish there was a way I could include a few of these "samples" up front.

I can't. But what I can promise here are recipes that are so easy and fun to make and so satisfying to taste that they will get raves from even your harshest critics—members of your own family.

One of the great joys of pan cooking is getting to sample your creations as you go along, first, for the very practical purpose of adjusting flavors, but mostly because it's simply impossible not to.

In addition to taste, I also admit to a weakness for recipes that make the whole house smell good. Check out, for instance, the recipe for Too Many Tomatoes and Sweet Sausage Tomato Sauce (page 226). When reheated, this dish gives off such a homey aroma it could probably be repackaged and sold as a kitchen air freshener.

To assist me in my culinary adventures, I have enlisted the aid of Susan Wyler, a former editor of *Food and Wine* magazine and an award-winning cookbook author in her own right. Susan and I have also created over 100 cookbooks together including 365 *Ways to Cook* . . . (chicken, pasta, etc.), one of the best-selling cookbook series of all time.

With Susan's help I have learned to love cooking in my pan so much that I now use it for recipes that might be easier made in other types of cookware. I don't recommend throwing away all your other cookware, but I do hope this book will inspire you to feel the same way about your pan that I feel about mine.

Below are some obligatory topics that need to be covered in a book of this sort. Please don't skip over them (feel free to scan if you must): there's information here that might actually come in handy.

CHOOSING YOUR PAN

The rule of thumb for buying a frying pan is the same as for buying a house: you don't want to buy the cheapest house on the block, but you don't want to buy the most expensive one either.

Pan nomenclature is inconsistent. One manufacturer's frying pan is another's skillet. One brand's 8-inch sauté pan is another's omelet pan. The pan I use, which is the one I am sitting in on the cover, is a Farberware "Millennium" nonstick sauté pan. I like it because it has high sides that will hold greater volume, it comes with a lid, the heat is evenly distributed, the bottom doesn't turn black, and it doesn't weigh 50 pounds. It retails for about $50.

You can spend more than twice as much for copper or certain specialized metal lines. You can also spend half as much, especially if you bargain shop at discount stores and buy the pan and lid separately. It really doesn't matter what you spend as long as your pan meets certain important criteria. When choosing a pan, there are four major considerations:

1. Make sure it's "nonstick." For me, the nonstick surface is the greatest culinary invention since the knife and fork. It's as though Brillo was invented for people who simply haven't gotten the word yet.

2. Choose a mid-priced pan. The nonstick surface of the cheaper pan doesn't last. At the other end of the spectrum—and maybe I'm just being an anti-snob here—I think the most expensive pans are an affectation.

3. Make sure it has a lid. Most frying pans and skillets (the ones with the sloped edges) do not come with lids. In most cookware and department stores, however, lids can be purchased separately. If none matches your pan exactly, ask for a "universal lid," which is notched so it can serve as a cover for several different-sized pans.

4. Road-test your pan. Pick it up, feel its weight, its balance. Imagine yourself flipping a flapjack. Do you feel more comfortable with straight or slanted edges? Is it the right size for the type or quantity of cooking you plan to do? The most popular pan size and the one assumed in all the recipes in this book is 12 inches—big enough to feed a family. You don't want a pan that's too heavy to lift, but if the bottom is too lightweight, the pan will not conduct heat evenly. In short, treat the pan as though you were trying out a new tennis racket or golf putter.

THE NONSTICK SURFACE

In 1962 the word *Teflon* entered the popular culture. For the home cook it was a godsend. But in terms of durability Teflon is to today's nonstick surfaces what the black and white TV is to satellite television. In the mid-1970s, Dupont introduced "Silverstone," which, to extend the metaphor, was comparable to the advent of color TV.

Today, the industry buzzwords for quality nonstick are "food release," meaning how efficiently the food releases from the pan and how little residue remains. As durable as today's nonstick surfaces are, even the best begin to lose some of their food-release quality over time.

The archenemies of the nonstick surface are extremely high heat and abrasion. In general, it is recommended that you use wood or plastic utensils with your nonstick pan. In truth, however, today's better nonstick surfaces are so durable, you will not ruin the coating of your pan with regular utensils if you use reasonable care.

TEMPERATURE

Restaurant chefs generally do all their pan cooking at one temperature: blowtorch. They simply cannot cook anything at less than hot, hot, hot and still manage to feed several hundred people a night. They do not have the luxury of using nonstick pans for this reason—excessive heat. You do, but you should also be aware of how temperature affects your pan and how you can control it.

The thing that most affects a pan's temperature is not the temperature setting, but what is in the pan itself. For instance, if you fill your pan with water, turn the heat to high, and continue to refill the pan as the water evaporates, it will boil along forever at just over 212 degrees F. On the other hand, an empty pan over high heat can go from 0 to 700 degrees F in a matter of minutes.

By the way, if you leave your empty nonstick pan on the stove over high heat for, say, an hour, it won't explode or melt, or anything like that. In fact, it will look exactly the same; it will just no longer be nonstick. Other elements that affect the temperature of a pan are the temperature setting, the metal composition, and the thickness and weight of the pan.

What does all this have to do with you? Two things. First and most obviously, you don't want to buy a new nonstick pan and immediately ruin its nonstick feature by overheating it. Second, when following a recipe, for the cooking time to be accurate, you need to have your pan maintain a somewhat consistent temperature.

Many of the recipes in this book call for cooking over high or medium-high heat. This is because these dishes need to be seared, or caramelized. Also, for deep frying, the hotter the oil, the less greasy the food. Generally, I tend to heat my pan for roughly two minutes before even adding any oil. This brings the surface temperature to about 400 degrees F. Different oils have different smoke points, but once I add the oil and before it starts to smoke, that's when I begin cooking.

OILS

You can cook in a nonstick pan with no oil without hurting your pan but probably spoiling whatever it is you're cooking. Surprisingly, vegetable oil sprays like Pam can actually hurt your pan in that they leave a hot residue right at the surface. If you do use an oil spray, it should be at moderate temperature or lower and not for any extended period of time.

Different fats have different smoke points. Butter has one of the lowest smoke points; safflower oil, one of the highest. As a general, all-purpose cooking oil, I use olive oil or canola oil. For deep frying, or even shallow frying, I use vegetable oil.

Most exotic or infused oils, such as walnut or truffle oil, are great on salads but a waste of money if used in cooking. On this same note, there are almost as many grades and qualities of olive oil in Italy as there are wines. Therefore, I keep two bottles of olive oil in the kitchen at all times: a fruitier higher-quality extra-virgin oil for salads and dipping and a less expensive pure olive oil, which actually has a higher smoke point, for cooking.

If you like a buttery flavor, but generally prefer to cut back on saturated fat and the taste of burned butter, start with olive oil and add a pat or two of butter to the heated oil just for flavor. The oil helps prevent the butter from burning, while the butter does not lower the smoke point of the oil—a double benefit!

TECHNIQUE

My pan technique is not the greatest. All right, it's somewhere between fair and poor. I tend to be a sloppy cook. My smoke detector goes off with alarming regularity. I seem to have a hard time cooking two things at once. And I once singed my eyebrows while flambéing a lamb chop.

I have a friend (and client), Bob Blumer, TV's "The Surreal Gourmet," who can toss and turn everything in his pan with a flick of the wrist without spilling a single particle of food. In contrast, whenever I try this chef's technique, I tend to lose about one-third of whatever it is that I am cooking. While my technique leaves something to be desired, I would like to report that I have discovered three amazing inventions: the spoon, the tongs, and the spatula.

A WOMAN AND HER PAN

I feel I need to close with a word about the *"Man"* part of *A Man and His Pan.* I suppose the name could have been *A Person and His or Her Pan,* but that seemed to lose something. In truth, this book is very personal and reflects the "guy way" I like to cook. Whether it's sautéing, flambéing, or frying, I really do believe men like to cook in frying pans: it's showy, it's a bit ego-driven in that it's kind of fun to add extra ingredients as you go along (therefore creating a dish that is totally original and utterly unreproducible), and it's okay to be a little messy. On the other side of that, nothing's easier to clean up than one nonstick pan.

But obviously, because of its ease and simplicity, how could pan cooking not appeal to women, particularly working women and women with children (often one in the same), who because of the multiple roles they need to play, have less time and more "on their plate" than most men do.

These recipes were designed to be enjoyed by anyone who is enthusiastic about cooking and eating. Many of them are more nutritious and less caloric than typical takeout, and they can be prepared and on the table in less time than it takes the Chinese food to arrive.

We now come to the point in any introductory cookbook chapter I've ever seen where it is time to wish you, the reader, "Bon appétit." But in the case of *A Man and His Pan,* I just don't feel that's adequate. Instead I'd like to close with the Cajun French phrase: *Laissez les bons temps rouler!* ("Let the good times roll!")

CHAPTER I
GREAT PAN BREAKFASTS: MORE THAN JUST EGGS

Eggs McBoswell

Mexican Scramble with Cheese, Chiles, and Salsa

Midnight Scrambler

Sunday Morning Vegetable Frittata

Spanish Potato and Onion Omelet

Smoked Salmon Scramble with Cream Cheese and Chives

Huevos Rancheros

Eggs Santa Fe in Pink Salsa Cream

Eggs Florentine with Smoked Salmon

Truck Stop Steak 'n' Eggs with Home-Fried Potatoes

Handkerchief Egg Crepes with Olive Filling

Easy Cheesy Pan Soufflé

Challah French Toast with Almond-Honey Butter

Whole-Grain French Toast with Warm Berry Compote

Three-Grain Griddle Cakes

Eggs McBoswell

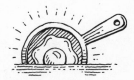

Prosciutto, a cured, unsmoked Italian ham, fries up beautifully (I first learned this amazing fact from a pizza I burned) with more taste and texture than American ham or Canadian bacon. It also requires no additional oil if cooked in a nonstick pan. For frying, buy domestic prosciutto; it's about half the price of imported.

2 ounces prosciutto, thinly sliced (a little goes a long way)
2 tablespoons butter
2 eggs
2 slices of Monterey Jack cheese or, if cooking for children, 4 slices of mild
**   Cheddar cheese or mild Italian cheese, like provolone or mozzarella**
2 English muffins, split in half
Mayonnaise

1. In your nonstick frying pan, fry the prosciutto over high heat, stirring frequently once the meat starts to sizzle, until crisp, 6 to 8 minutes. Set aside. Remove the pan from the heat to cool slightly.

2. Add 1 tablespoon butter to the pan and return to medium heat. Crack the eggs into the pan and fry until the yolks are set enough to flip, about 3 to 4 minutes. Flip the eggs and top each with 1 slice of cheese. Cover the pan and cook until the cheese melts, about 1 minute. With a wide spatula, carefully remove the eggs to a plate without breaking the yolks.

3. Melt the remaining butter in the pan. Add the English muffins and brown on both sides, a total of 1 to 2 minutes. Remove the muffins from the pan and spread them with mayonnaise to taste.

4. Place an egg with cheese on top of 2 of the English muffin halves. Place the prosciutto, evenly divided, on top of the eggs and cover with the remaining muffin halves to make a sandwich. Serve while the eggs are still warm.

SERVES 2

MEXICAN SCRAMBLE WITH CHEESE, CHILES, AND SALSA

This hearty scramble is based on the Mexican dish called *migas*. Frugally designed to use up leftover corn tortillas, it's just as good made with tortilla chips. The chips mostly melt into the creamy eggs, leaving behind a bit of texture and their delicious corn flavor. The eggs are also great as a casual late supper.

12 eggs
¾ teaspoon salt
½ teaspoon freshly ground pepper
3 tablespoons unsalted butter
⅓ cup drained chopped canned or frozen hot green chiles
24 corn tortilla chips
4 ounces grated Monterey Jack cheese (1 heaping cup)
Salsa, for serving

1. In a large bowl, whisk the eggs briefly, for streaky results, or thoroughly, for homogeneous results. Whisk in the salt and pepper.

2. In your nonstick frying pan, melt the butter over medium heat. When it foams, add the chiles. Cook, uncovered, stirring once or twice, for 5 minutes. Add the eggs and chips and cook, stirring often and scraping the eggs up from the bottom of the pan as they set, until the chips are fairly soggy and the eggs are done to your liking, about 4 minutes for medium-firm eggs. Stir the cheese into the eggs, remove from the heat, cover, and let stand for 30 seconds.

3. Divide the eggs among 4 warmed plates and serve immediately, accompanied with salsa for dolloping on at the table.

SERVES 4

MIDNIGHT SCRAMBLER

This is a great pick-me-up after a too-long evening on the town. Since the main ingredients are mixed together in a can there is little cleaning up to do.

3 eggs
2 tablespoons milk
I teaspoon Worcestershire sauce
½ teaspoon garlic salt or celery salt
5 drops of Tabasco sauce
I can (14½ ounces) stewed tomatoes, drained
I tablespoon unsalted butter

1. In a small bowl, mix together the eggs and milk until blended but not bubbly; set aside.

2. Add the Worcestershire sauce, garlic salt, and the Tabasco sauce directly to the can of tomatoes and stir. (I actually "stir" with a pair of scissors, further slicing up the stewed tomatoes as I go.)

3. In your nonstick frying pan, melt the butter over high heat. When the butter is foamy, pour in the eggs. Reduce the heat to medium and cook the eggs, pushing them gently around the pan with a spatula, until barely set, about 30 seconds. Add the tomato mixture and continue to cook while stirring for another 2 to 3 minutes. Immediately transfer to a plate and serve.

SERVES 2

Sunday Morning Vegetable Frittata

I call this Sunday morning frittata, because I usually make it with the vegetables left over from our Saturday night dinner parties. The following is merely a blueprint; you can adjust it according to what you have on hand. Just be sure there is about one cup of cubed or sliced cooked potatoes and at least one onion as a base.

1 cup leftover cooked diced potatoes or 2 medium red potatoes
2 tablespoons olive oil
1 medium onion, cut into ½-inch dice
Salt and freshly ground pepper
2 garlic cloves, chopped
½ green bell pepper, cut into ½-inch dice
½ red bell pepper, cut into ½-inch dice
8 eggs, lightly beaten
½ cup cooked broccoli or cauliflower florets
1 plum tomato, sliced
2 ounces cream cheese, at room temperature

1. If you don't have leftover cooked potatoes, either wrap the potatoes in wet paper towels and microwave them on high for 1½ to 2 minutes, turning once halfway through, or boil them for 5 to 7 minutes, until barely tender. As soon as they are cool enough to handle, peel the potatoes and cut them into ½-inch dice.

2. In your nonstick frying pan, heat the olive oil over medium-high heat. Add the onion and cook until softened and translucent, about 3 minutes. Add the potatoes and cook, stirring, until they are lightly browned and the onion is golden, 3 to 5 minutes longer. Season generously with salt and pepper.

3. Add the garlic and the green and red bell peppers to the pan. Cook, stirring often, until the peppers are slightly softened but still brightly colored, 2 to 3 minutes longer.

4. Season the eggs with about ¼ teaspoon each salt and pepper. Pour them into the pan, tilting to distribute them evenly. Reduce the heat to medium-low. Arrange the broccoli florets on top, pushing them gently down into the eggs. Distribute the tomato slices around the frittata and dollop the cream cheese in between. Cover, reduce the heat to low, and cook until the eggs are firm and puffed around the edges though still slightly runny in the center.

5. Carefully slide the frittata out onto a round platter or large plate, then invert it back into the pan. Cook, uncovered, until the eggs are completely set, 2 to 3 minutes. Serve hot, warm, or at room temperature.

SERVES 4 TO 6

Spanish Potato and Onion Omelet

In Spain this is called a *tortilla de patata,* but it's not a tortilla at all; it's a thick, firm omelet, chock-full of tasty fried potatoes and onions. I like this dish because it's good hot, at room temperature, or cold. It's appropriate for breakfast, lunch, or a between-meal snack. Cut into little pieces, it makes a fine pass-around appetizer.

¼ cup fruity olive oil
1 large onion, cut into ½-inch dice
1 pound red potatoes, peeled and cut into ½-inch dice
8 eggs
½ teaspoon salt
¼ teaspoon freshly ground pepper
⅛ teaspoon Tabasco or other hot sauce

1. In your nonstick frying pan, heat the olive oil over medium-high heat. Add the onion and cook, stirring, for 1 minute. Add the potatoes and cook, stirring and turning the potatoes over with a spatula, 2 minutes longer. Cover the pan, reduce the heat to medium-low, and cook, stirring and turning the potatoes occasionally, until they are browned and tender, 7 to 10 minutes longer.

2. Meanwhile, in a medium bowl, beat the eggs until blended. Season with the salt, pepper, and Tabasco. When the potatoes are tender, pour the eggs into the pan. Quickly stir, scraping up the potatoes and onions from the bottom to distribute the ingredients evenly. Cover again, reduce the heat to low, and cook until the eggs are firm and puffed around the edges though still slightly runny in the center.

3. Carefully slide the omelet out onto a round platter or large plate, then invert it back into the pan. Cook, uncovered, until the omelet is completely set, about 3 minutes. Cut into wedges to serve.

SERVES 4 TO 6

Smoked Salmon Scramble with Cream Cheese and Chives

This has almost all the elements of a great breakfast or brunch. It's only missing one element, which you can fill in easily—warm toasted bagels! Serve with freshly squeezed orange juice and strong, freshly brewed coffee.

8 eggs
I tablespoon minced fresh dill or ½ teaspoon dried tarragon
¼ teaspoon salt
¼ teaspoon freshly ground pepper
Several drops of hot sauce
3 tablespoons unsalted butter
2 ounces cream cheese with chives, at room temperature
3 to 4 ounces thinly sliced smoked salmon, preferably Scottish or Norwegian but Nova will do, cut into thin strips

1. In a mixing bowl, beat the eggs with the dill, salt, pepper, and hot sauce until the yolks and whites are blended.

2. In your nonstick frying pan, melt 3 tablespoons of the butter over medium heat. Pour in the eggs and immediately reduce the heat to medium-low. Cook, stirring the eggs and scraping the bottom of the pan, until the eggs become creamy, about 2 minutes.

3. As the eggs begin to set, push them into small mounds. Reduce the heat to low and quickly dollop the cream cheese over the eggs. Stir gently to partially melt the cheese and mix it unevenly around the curds of egg.

4. At the very last minute, add the smoked salmon to the pan and fold gently to mix everything together while leaving discrete soft pillows of egg. Serve at once.

SERVES 3 OR 4

Huevos Rancheros

Traditionally, the eggs for this spicy Tex-Mex breakfast classic are cooked sunny-side up. If you think that sounds too much like rush hour at the cantina, the eggs can be scrambled instead and the dish will still taste great. For best flavor, make the sauce the night before. For not quite as fine flavor but less work, skip to step 2 and use 1 cup prepared red enchilada sauce.

1½ tablespoons olive oil
½ cup chopped onion
1 jalapeño pepper, minced (include the seeds and ribs for a spicier sauce)
2 garlic cloves, minced
¼ teaspoon dried oregano
1 can (7 ounces) chopped green chiles, drained
½ cup canned crushed tomatoes with added puree
½ cup reduced-sodium canned chicken broth
¼ teaspoon salt
3 to 4 tablespoons corn oil
4 (6- to 7-inch) corn tortillas
1 can (16 ounces) refried beans
2 tablespoons unsalted butter
8 eggs
2½ ounces feta cheese, crumbled

1. In your nonstick frying pan, warm the olive oil over low heat. Add the onion, jalapeño, garlic, and oregano. Cover and cook, stirring once or twice, for 5 minutes. Add the chiles, tomatoes, broth, and salt. Bring to a simmer. Partially cover and cook until thick, 6 to 8 minutes. Remove to a bowl and rinse out the pan. If preparing the sauce in advance, let cool, then cover and refrigerate.

2. Set your pan over medium heat. Add the corn oil. When it is hot, add the tortillas one at a time, and cook, turning once, until flexible and tender, 20 to

30 seconds per side; the tortillas should not become crisp. Drain the tortillas on paper towels. Wipe the pan with a paper towel.

3. Warm the refried beans in a small heavy saucepan or in a glass bowl in a microwave, stirring often. Reheat the sauce, if necessary.

4. Set your pan over medium-low heat. Add the butter and when it is foaming, crack the eggs in pairs into the pan. Cover and cook until the whites are just set, about 4 minutes. Season lightly with additional salt.

5. Set each tortilla on a heated plate. Spread the hot refried beans generously over the tortillas. With a spatula, set each pair of eggs atop a tortilla. Spoon the sauce over the eggs. Sprinkle the feta over the sauce and serve immediately.

SERVES 4

Eggs Santa Fe in Pink Salsa Cream

This luscious dish is a New Mexican take on eggs Benedict. Poached free-form in a skillet of simmering water (a low-fat technique definitely worth mastering), the eggs are served atop corn bread squares and napped with a spicy pink sauce. Serve this brunch creation with fresh juices or mix up a batch of Tequila Sunrises.

8 very fresh eggs
I cup heavy cream
¾ cup spicy, tomato-based prepared salsa
I small garlic clove, crushed through a press
Salt
I cup freshly grated Parmesan cheese
I tablespoon distilled white vinegar
4 (4-inch) squares of leftover corn bread or English muffins, split and lightly
**   toasted**
Thin slices of avocado and sprigs of cilantro, as garnish (optional)

1. Fill your nonstick frying pan three-quarters full of water and bring to a boil over high heat. Using a slotted spoon, one at a time, lower each egg in its shell into the boiling water; leave for 8 seconds, rolling gently to briefly immerse all sides, then transfer to an absorbent cloth. Let cool. Set the pan of water aside off heat.

2. In a heavy medium nonreactive saucepan, combine the cream, salsa, garlic, and a pinch of salt. Bring to a boil over medium heat and cook, stirring occasionally, until it begins to thicken, about 7 minutes. Stir in the Parmesan cheese. Remove the salsa cream from the heat and cover to keep warm.

3. Meanwhile, bring the pan of water to a gentle simmer. Add the vinegar (you won't taste the vinegar, but it helps the eggs set). One at a time, holding each egg just above the surface, crack the eggs into the water. Cook, moving the eggs gently with a spoon to promote even cooking, without ever letting the water bubble briskly, until the poached eggs are done to your liking, about 4 minutes for soft eggs.

4. Set 2 corn bread slices on each of 4 plates. With a slotted spoon, lift the eggs, one at a time, from the water. Blot gently on an absorbent towel, then set 1 egg atop each corn bread slice. Spoon the salsa cream sauce over and around the eggs. Garnish each plate with avocado slices and cilantro sprigs, if desired, and serve immediately.

SERVES 4

EGGS FLORENTINE WITH SMOKED SALMON

Good as classic eggs Florentine are (eggs topped with a creamy spinach sauce), they're even better when that sauce incorporates smoked salmon. Here the salmon is the hot-smoked (Alaskan, Pacific Northwestern, etc.) variety, and the fish is flaked directly into the sauce. Alternately, use good-quality cold-smoked salmon (such as Scottish), and arrange thin slices over the muffins but under the eggs, like Canadian bacon in eggs Benedict. Either way, poach the eggs free-form in your indispensable 12-inch skillet.

8 very fresh eggs
1 tablespoon butter
1 tablespoon flour
1 cup milk
½ teaspoon salt
¼ cup heavy cream
2 teaspoons Dijon mustard
8 ounces frozen chopped spinach, thawed and squeezed dry
2 ounces dry-smoked salmon, skinned if necessary and flaked
Freshly ground pepper
1 tablespoon distilled white vinegar
4 English muffins, split and lightly toasted
½ cup freshly grated Parmesan cheese

1. Fill your nonstick frying pan three-quarters full of water and bring to a boil over high heat. Using a slotted spoon, one at a time, lower each egg in its shell into the boiling water; leave for 8 seconds, rolling gently to briefly immerse all sides, then transfer to an absorbent cloth. Let cool.

2. In a heavy medium saucepan, melt the butter over low heat. Whisk in the flour and cook, uncovered, whisking often without browning, for 2 minutes.

Gradually whisk in the milk. Raise the heat and bring the mixture to a boil, whisking until thick and smooth. Reduce the heat to medium-low and simmer, whisking occasionally and scraping the bottom of the pan, for 3 minutes. Whisk in the salt, cream, and mustard, then stir in the spinach and salmon. Season generously with pepper. Remove from the heat and cover to keep warm.

3. Meanwhile, bring the pan of water to a gentle simmer. Add the vinegar (you won't taste the vinegar, but it helps the eggs set). One at a time, holding each egg just above the surface, crack the eggs into the water. Cook, moving the eggs gently with a spoon to promote even cooking, without ever letting the water bubble briskly, until the poached eggs are done to your liking, about 4 minutes for soft eggs.

4. Preheat the broiler. Set the toasted muffin halves in each of 4 shallow, flame-proof individual serving dishes. With a slotted spoon, remove the eggs from the water. Blot gently on an absorbent towel, then set 1 egg atop each muffin half. Spoon the spinach mixture over the eggs, spreading to completely mask the eggs. Sprinkle the Parmesan cheese evenly over the top.

5. Working in batches if necessary, set the dishes of eggs under the broiler about 6 inches from the heat and cook until golden brown and bubbling, 1 to 2 minutes. Serve immediately.

SERVES 4

Truck Stop Steak 'n' Eggs with Home-Fried Potatoes

Some mornings you just feel like making breakfast a major meal. Maybe it's Mother's Day, and Dad or the kids want to give Mom a treat. Or maybe you've got a big day ahead and want to fuel up. Whatever the motivation, the whole trick to preparing this substantial meal in one pan is in the timing. Since they take the most time, the home fries have to be cooked first. Then the steak is started. I like to cook up one thick steak and slice it. The two minutes it rests before being sliced are used to prepare the eggs. Here's how it goes.

1 boneless rib, shell, or strip steak, cut 1 inch thick (¾ to 1 pound), trimmed
    of all excess fat
1 garlic clove, cut in half
2 teaspoons Worcestershire sauce
Salt and freshly ground pepper
2 large red potatoes, cooked and peeled (use leftovers or microwave pota-
    toes for 2 to 3 minutes on high until just tender)
3½ tablespoons olive oil or other vegetable oil
1 small onion, coarsely chopped
1½ tablespoons butter
4 eggs
Steak sauce

1. Rub the steak with the cut sides of the garlic. Brush the steak on both sides with the Worcestershire sauce. Season with salt and pepper. Set aside at room temperature. Quarter the potatoes, then cut into ¼- to ⅜-inch-thick slices.

2. In your nonstick frying pan, heat 2 tablespoons of the oil over medium-high heat. Add the onion and potatoes. Cook, tossing for 1 to 2 minutes to lightly coat the potatoes with oil. Then continue to cook, turning only occasionally,

until the slices are nicely browned, about 5 minutes. Season generously with salt and pepper. Remove to a bowl, cover with foil, and set aside.

3. Wipe the pan clean; no need to rinse. Add the remaining oil to the pan and set over medium-high heat for about 1 minute. Add the steak, cover, and cook undisturbed for 3 minutes, until browned on the bottom. Turn over, cover, reduce the heat to medium, and cook until browned on the second side and rare or medium-rare in the center, 3 to 4 minutes, or a minute or two longer to desired degree of doneness. Remove the steak to a cutting board. Pour off the oil and wipe out the pan.

4. Add the butter to the pan and set over medium heat. Some people like their steak and eggs with sunny-side up eggs; others prefer scrambled. Cook the eggs as you prefer. Cut the steak crosswise on an angle into wide slices, reserving any juices. If necessary, reheat the potatoes quickly in the pan. Plate the steak and eggs and pile on some home fries. Pour any juices from the sliced steak over the meat and potatoes and serve at once. Pass steak sauce on the side.

SERVES 2

HANDKERCHIEF EGG CREPES WITH OLIVE FILLING

For grown-ups only! This is a sophisticated egg dish that can serve perfectly either as an intimate breakfast for two or as a late-night snack. I make it with olive spread, also called olive tapenade, available in a jar at the supermarket. Some olive pastes contain walnuts, which would be fine here. Note that I give a range of amounts to add, because different brands vary in intensity. You could also substitute any kind of caviar for the olive spread, in which case some minced fresh chives would be nice as well. Accompany these delicate crepes with toasted brioche or croissants.

2 ounces cream cheese,* at room temperature
2 tablespoons sour cream
2 to 3 tablespoons jarred black olive spread or paste, to taste
4 eggs
2 tablespoons milk
¼ teaspoon salt
Dash of cayenne
3 tablespoons unsalted butter

1. In a small bowl, combine the softened cream cheese and sour cream. Blend well. Stir in enough of the olive spread so that the filling is intensely flavored but not overpowering.

2. In a mixing bowl, beat the eggs with a fork until they are blended but still streaked. Beat in the milk until well blended. Season with the salt and cayenne.

3. In your nonstick frying pan, melt about 2 teaspoons of the butter over medium heat. Ladle ¼ to ⅓ cup of the beaten eggs into the pan. Swirl so that the eggs cover most of the bottom fairly evenly in a thin layer. Cover and cook 45

to 60 seconds, until the crepe is just set. Slide onto a plate. Repeat with the remaining butter and eggs to make 3 more crepes.

4. As the crepes are done, dollop one-fourth of the filling onto the center. Fold
in half, then in half again to make large triangles. Arrange 2 crepes, overlapping
slightly, on each plate. Serve at once.

*You can use reduced-fat cream cheese, sometimes called Neufchâtel, here, but
this is not the place for nonfat cheese, which does not soften well.

SERVES 2

Easy Cheesy Pan Soufflé

What makes this so easy is not having to prepare a soufflé mold and collar and not having to worry about the finished dish falling like a ton of bricks. Made in the pan, the soufflé puffs impressively but without the height and drama it would have in a deep soufflé dish; conversely, it is firmer and holds up surprisingly well.

For best flavor, I like to use a combination of Gruyère and Parmesan cheeses. You can substitute all Gruyère, Swiss, or Cheddar if you prefer. The only trick here is to regulate the heat so that the soufflé steams in the pan, puffing considerably before the bottom browns; then it is transferred to the oven to finish cooking.

4 tablespoons butter
3 tablespoons flour
I cup milk
¼ teaspoon salt
⅛ teaspoon grated nutmeg
Dash of cayenne, or more to taste
3 egg yolks
¾ cup shredded Gruyère cheese
¼ cup grated imported Parmesan cheese
4 egg whites

1. Preheat the oven to 400 degrees F. In a heavy medium saucepan, melt 3 tablespoons of the butter over medium heat. Add the flour and cook, stirring, for 1 to 2 minutes without allowing the mixture to brown. Gradually whisk in the milk and bring to a boil, whisking until smooth and thickened, about 1 minute. Mix in the salt, nutmeg, and cayenne. Remove from the heat.

2. One at a time, beat in the egg yolks, whisking until completely blended. Add the Gruyère and Parmesan cheese to the hot sauce, stirring until melted and smooth.

3. In a clean bowl, beat the egg whites until stiff but not dry. Dollop a big spoonful of the egg whites onto the warm cheese base. Stir to mix in and lighten the base. Gently fold in the rest of the beaten egg whites, being careful not to deflate the mixture. If in doubt, underblend rather than overmix.

4. If your nonstick frying pan does not have a metal handle, wrap the handle in several thicknesses of aluminum foil, shiny side out. Melt the remaining butter in the pan over medium heat, swirling to coat the bottom and sides. Scrape the soufflé into the pan and cover tightly with a lid. Cook for 2 minutes. Reduce the heat to medium-low and cook 5 minutes longer without peeking. After the full 7 minutes, check the soufflé. It should be risen and firm around the sides but still soft in the center.

5. Transfer the pan to the preheated oven. Bake for 5 to 7 minutes, or until the soufflé is puffed and just set. Serve at once. Either serve from the pan, cutting the soufflé into wedges and presenting them browned side up, or invert onto a large round platter.

SERVES 4

CHALLAH FRENCH TOAST WITH ALMOND-HONEY BUTTER

The fine-grained, golden-braided bread called challah makes superior French toast, soaking up the eggy custard and cooking up as rich and tender as the finest of bread puddings. Like pancakes, French toast doesn't really fry, it bakes—just a spritz of nonstick spray is all you need. Organized types will want to make the sweet and crunchy nut butter the night before, in order to get this great breakfast treat on the table ASAP.

5 tablespoons unsalted butter, softened slightly
¼ cup chopped toasted almonds
3 tablespoons honey
5 eggs, thoroughly beaten
1¼ cups milk
1 tablespoon sugar
4 large slices of challah or other egg bread, cut about 1¼ inches thick
Confectioners' sugar, in a sieve

1. In a small bowl, mix together the butter, almonds, and honey. If not using immediately, cover the almond-honey butter and refrigerate. Soften it at room temperature before using.

2. In a large shallow baking dish, whisk together the beaten eggs, milk, and sugar. Add the bread slices and let them soak, turning occasionally, until they are well saturated.

3. Coat your nonstick frying pan lightly but evenly with nonstick cooking spray and set over medium heat. One at a time, lift the bread slices from the milk mixture, letting the excess drip back into the dish. Lay the slices in the pan, lower the heat slightly, and cook, uncovered, rearranging the slices in the pan to

promote even cooking and turning them once, until they are crisp, golden brown, and custardy but not wet inside, 5 to 7 minutes total.

4. Transfer the French toast to plates. Dust heavily with confectioners' sugar. Top each slice with a dollop of the almond butter, dividing it evenly and using it all. Serve immediately.

SERVES 4

WHOLE-GRAIN FRENCH TOAST WITH WARM BERRY COMPOTE

As with the challah French toast, it takes a thick slice of whole-grain bread to stay moist and custardy after cooking. Sandwich-sliced breads are cut too thin; buy an unsliced loaf instead and cut it yourself with a serrated knife. The fruit topping uses frozen berries, making it a spontaneous, all-season treat. Come summer, use fresh berries for an even more delicious result.

1½ cups frozen unsweetened strawberries, thawed slightly and halved
1 cup frozen blueberries
⅓ cup genuine maple syrup
⅓ cup fresh orange juice
2 teaspoons arrowroot or cornstarch
2 tablespoons unsalted butter, softened
5 eggs, thoroughly beaten
1¼ cups milk
1 tablespoon sugar
4 large slices of whole-grain bread, cut 1¼ inches thick
Confectioners' sugar

1. In a medium nonreactive saucepan, combine the strawberries, blueberries, maple syrup, and ¼ cup orange juice. In a small bowl, stir together the remaining orange juice and the arrowroot. Set the saucepan over medium heat, cover, and bring to a simmer. Uncover and cook, stirring occasionally, until thickened slightly, about 4 minutes. Stir in the arrowroot mixture and remove from the heat. Let stand, stirring once or twice, until thick, about 30 seconds. Stir in the butter until smooth. Cover and keep warm until using. Do not reheat or stir any more than necessary or the compote may thin.

2. In a large shallow baking dish, whisk together the beaten eggs, milk, and sugar. Add the bread slices and let soak, turning occasionally, until well saturated.

3. Coat your nonstick frying pan lightly but evenly with nonstick spray and set over medium heat. One at a time, lift the bread slices from the milk mixture, letting the excess drip back. Lay the slices in the pan, lower the heat slightly, and cook, uncovered, rearranging the slices in the pan to promote even cooking and turning them once, until they are crisp, golden brown, and custardy but not wet inside, 5 to 7 minutes total.

4. Transfer the slices to plates. Dust heavily with confectioners' sugar. Spoon the berry compote generously over the French toast and serve immediately.

SERVES 4

THREE-GRAIN GRIDDLE CAKES

Pancakes are one of kids' favorite breakfast foods. On Sundays, we occasionally serve them for supper as a special treat. These griddle cakes made with a variety of grains are a good way to provide a little extra fiber and nutrition. Serve with thin pats of butter and plenty of maple syrup.

1¼ **cups flour**
½ **cup yellow cornmeal**
⅓ **cup buckwheat flour**
1½ **tablespoons sugar**
1 **teaspoon baking powder**
¾ **teaspoon baking soda**
¼ **teaspoon salt**
2 **eggs**
2 **cups buttermilk**
4 **tablespoons unsalted butter, melted**

1. In a medium bowl, combine the all-purpose flour, cornmeal, buckwheat flour, sugar, baking powder, baking soda, and salt. Mix well.

2. In a large glass measure or another bowl, whisk the eggs and buttermilk until well blended. Add the liquids to the dry ingredients and stir to partially mix. Stir in the melted butter, mixing until the batter is just barely blended. There should be small lumps remaining. Do not overmix.

3. Grease your nonstick frying pan lightly and set it over medium heat for about 1 minute. Ladle about 3 tablespoons of the batter into the pan for each cake, spreading it out to a 3- to 4-inch diameter. You will be able to fit 3 or 4 in the pan at a time. Cook until the bottoms are nicely browned and the tops have little bubbles all over them, 1½ to 2 minutes. Gently turn the griddle cakes over

with a wide spatula and cook until the second sides are browned and the cakes are dry throughout, 45 to 60 seconds longer. Repeat with the remaining batter, greasing the pan when it looks dry. (Even if they wouldn't stick without it, this helps promote browning.) If the cakes start browning too fast, reduce the heat slightly. Serve hot.

SERVES 4 TO 6

CHAPTER 2

STEAKS AND CHOPS: THE MEAT OF THE MATTER

Thomas's Pan-Fried Steak with Madeira-Balsamic
 Reduction

Three-Peppercorn Steak au Poivre

Pepper-Crusted Pan Steak Flambéed in Whisky

Steak Pizzaiola

Gaucho Steak with Chimichurri Sauce

A Tiny-Bit-Sweet Pan-Roasted Pot Roast

Picadillo with Raisins, Olives, and Almonds

Veal Scaloppine with Lemon Vodka Sauce

Rosemary Veal Chops with Quick Pan Sauce

Pan-Grilled Pork Chops with Almost-Instant Apricot Chutney

Pork, Apples, and Prunes in Bourbon Cream Sauce

Quick Skillet Choucroute

Sausages and Peppers

Country Spareribs Braised with Bacon and Beer

Lamb Chops with Pernod

Lamb Chops Sautéed with Sweet Peppers and Olives

Glazed Ham Steaks with Raisin Sauce

Thomas's Pan-Fried Steak with Madeira-Balsamic Reduction

This fabulous recipe was given to me by my friend Thomas Wilson, a New York bartender and actor, who knows as much about food as he does about mixed drinks. It's one of his simple, can't-miss steak dishes. The pepper and mustard help cut the sweetness of the Madeira and balsamic vinegar.

2 boneless shell or Delmonico steaks (12 ounces each), cut 1 inch thick
1 teaspoon salt
2 teaspoons coarsely cracked pepper
1 tablespoon olive oil
2 tablespoons unsalted butter
2 medium shallots, thinly sliced
¾ cup Madeira wine
¼ cup balsamic vinegar
1 tablespoon Dijon mustard

1. Season the steaks liberally with the salt and pepper. In your nonstick frying pan, heat the olive oil over high heat. Add the steaks and cook to the desired doneness, 3½ to 4 minutes per side for rare, 6 to 7 minutes for well done. While they are cooking, press the steaks down with a spatula to help sear and brown the surfaces. Remove the steaks to a plate.

2. Add 1 tablespoon of the butter to the pan and melt over medium heat. Stir in the shallots and cook for about 30 seconds. Pour in the Madeira and balsamic vinegar. Boil over high heat, stirring, until reduced by half, 3 to 4 minutes. Whisk in the mustard until blended.

3. Remove the pan from the heat and whisk in the remaining 1 tablespoon butter until it just melts. Season the sauce with additional salt and pepper to taste. Pour the sauce over the steaks and serve at once.

SERVES 4

THREE-PEPPERCORN STEAK AU POIVRE

For a three-peppercorn steak, I mix black, white, and green peppercorns. If you have one of those fancy peppercorn mixes that contains red peppercorns and allspice berries as well, by all means use that and just rename this "Five-Peppercorn Steak."

4 boneless rib or Delmonico steaks (6 to 8 ounces each), cut ¾ inch thick
2 teaspoons coarse salt
1 tablespoon black peppercorns
1 teaspoon white peppercorns
1 teaspoon dried green peppercorns
2½ tablespoons olive oil
2 tablespoons butter
1 medium shallot, minced
¼ cup Cognac or brandy
½ cup heavy cream
1 teaspoon fresh lemon juice

1. Trim any external fat from the steaks. In a spice grinder or mini-food processor, process the salt and the black, white, and green peppercorns until they are coarsely ground. Mix the pepper-salt with 1 tablespoon of the olive oil. Smear this paste all over the steaks. Set them between 2 sheets of waxed paper or plastic wrap and let stand at room temperature for 1 to 2 hours.

2. When the rest of the meal is ready and you're all ready for your steaks, heat your nonstick frying pan over high heat. Add the remaining 1½ tablespoons oil and reduce the heat to medium-high. Add the steaks to the pan and sauté for 2 minutes on each side. Reduce the heat to medium and cook until rare or medium-rare, 3 to 5 minutes on each side, or longer to desired degree of doneness. Remove to warm plates.

3. Pour the oil from the pan and melt the butter in its place. Add the shallot and cook over medium heat until softened but not browned, about 1 minute. Pour in the Cognac and boil, scraping up any browned bits from the bottom of the pan, until it is reduced to 2 tablespoons, about 1 minute. Add the cream and lemon juice and boil until reduced by half, about 2 minutes. Season the sauce with salt and pepper to taste and spoon over the steaks. Serve at once.

SERVES 4

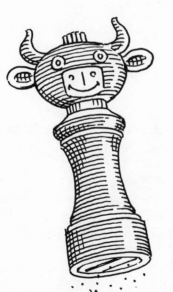

Pepper-Crusted Pan Steak
Flambéed in Whisky

Scotch and steak are natural partners. The smokiness of the liquor complements the charred steak perfectly and adds a deep note of flavor that will be a mystery unless you give out your secret. Here I sear the steak in the pan first, then cook it almost through. After slicing, the meat is returned to the pan and flambéed in most dramatic fashion.

2 boneless rib steaks (1 to 1¼ pounds each), cut 1½ inches thick
1½ tablespoons black peppercorns
2 teaspoons coarse salt
1 teaspoon herbes de Provence
¼ cup plus 1 tablespoon Scotch whisky
2½ tablespoons olive oil
2 tablespoons butter

1. Trim any excess fat you can off the meat. Set the steaks in a baking dish just large enough to hold them in a single layer.

2. In a spice grinder or with a mortar and pestle, grind together the peppercorns, salt, and herbes de Provence until the peppercorns are coarsely ground. Transfer to a small bowl and stir in 1 tablespoon each of the whisky and olive oil. Rub this spice paste all over the steaks. Set aside at room temperature to marinate for 1 hour.

3. Heat your nonstick frying pan over high heat for 1 minute. Add the remaining 1½ tablespoons oil and heat 1 minute longer. Add the steaks, cover, and cook until the bottom is brown, about 3 minutes. Turn over and cook the second side, uncovered, until browned on the bottom and rare inside, 3 to 5 minutes. Remove the steaks to a cutting board and let stand for at least 10 minutes.

4. Carve the meat against the grain on a sharp angle into 3 slices. The rarer you like your meat, the thicker the slices should be. Just before serving, melt the butter in the pan over medium heat. Return the steak slices to the skillet. Immediately pour the ¼ cup Scotch whisky into the pan, keeping your face averted, because sometimes it catches on its own. Carefully ignite with a match and shake the pan until the flames subside. Serve at once or cook 1 to 2 minutes longer if you want the meat well done. Serve the steak with the pan juices poured over the slices.

SERVES 4

Steak Pizzaiola

The *pizzaiola* is the man who makes the pizza, and so you would expect a dish named in his honor to include tomatoes, cheese, and maybe some of the more common pizza-topping vegetables like mushrooms and bell peppers. Maintain the pleasant fantasy that this is somehow baked in the pizza oven, while actually doing it all in your trusty pan. Serve a skinny pasta, like spaghettini, tossed with garlic and olive oil on the side, to mingle with the zesty sauce.

2 tablespoons olive oil
I large green or red bell pepper, cut into long, thin strips
4 garlic cloves, coarsely chopped
6 ounces cremini (brown) or white mushrooms, thickly sliced
Salt
¼ teaspoon crushed hot red pepper
I large thick New York steak (about I pound), at room temperature
½ cup dry red wine
I cup good-quality plain tomato sauce, such as marinara
¼ pound shredded processed provolone cheese
3 tablespoons finely chopped Italian flat-leaf parsley

1. Set your nonstick frying pan over medium-high heat. When it is hot, add the olive oil. When the oil is hot, add the bell pepper and garlic. Sauté, tossing and stirring often, until lightly colored, about 3 minutes.

2. Add the mushrooms, ¼ teaspoon salt, and the hot pepper. Cover the pan and cook, stirring once or twice, until the mushrooms begin to give up their juices, about 3 minutes. Transfer the vegetables to a bowl, scraping out all the flavored oil along with them. Clean and dry the pan. (The recipe can be prepared to this point several hours in advance.)

3. Pat the steak dry. Set the pan over high heat. When the pan is very hot, add the steak. Cook undisturbed for 5 minutes. Turn the steak over and cook until done to your liking (another 4 minutes or so for very rare); the steak will cook a bit further after it is combined with the sauce. Transfer to a cutting board.

4. Off heat, add the bell pepper mixture to the pan and stir well. Add the wine; it will bubble vigorously. Stir in the tomato sauce. Set the pan over low heat and bring the sauce to a simmer. Partially cover and simmer for 2 to 3 minutes to blend the flavors. Season with salt to taste.

5. Meanwhile, carve the steak across the grain and at a slight angle into thick slices. Season lightly with salt. Transfer to the skillet and fan the slices over the sauce. Top the steak with the cheese, cover the pan, and cook until the cheese melts, 2 to 3 minutes. Sprinkle with parsley and serve at once.

SERVES 2

Gaucho Steak with Chimichurri Sauce

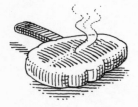

If you eat steak the way Argentineans eat steak, this Argentine-inspired dish may serve only two. For such carnivores, the sauce may seem beside the point, but in fact this emerald-hued parsley vinaigrette is the delicious secret weapon here. Serve plenty of good bread—mopping the plate of mingled chimichurri and steak juices makes a divine end to the meal.

2 tablespoons olive oil
1 tablespoon red wine vinegar
1 garlic clove, crushed through a press
½ teaspoon dried oregano
¼ teaspoon freshly ground pepper
1 flank steak (about 1½ pounds)
Salt
Chimichurri Sauce (recipe follows)

1. In a shallow nonreactive dish, stir together the olive oil, vinegar, garlic, oregano, and pepper. Add the steak and let it stand at room temperature, turning occasionally, for 1 hour.

2. Set your nonstick frying pan over high heat. When it is very hot, lift the steak from the marinade and lay it in the pan. Cook for 5 minutes, or until nicely browned. Scrape any marinade remaining in the dish onto the steak, turn it over, and cook until done to your liking, another 4 minutes or so for medium-rare.

3. Transfer to a cutting board and let rest for 5 minutes. Carve the steak across the grain and at a slight angle into thin slices. Season with salt to taste and serve. Pass the Chimichurri Sauce on the side.

SERVES 4

CHIMICHURRI SAUCE

Be sure to use the more flavorful flat-leaf variety of parsley for this verdant sauce. It will keep a few days in the refrigerator but is really best the same day it is made.

I cup lightly packed coarsely chopped Italian flat-leaf parsley
4 garlic cloves, chopped
4 teaspoons red wine vinegar
½ teaspoon salt
¼ teaspoon freshly ground pepper
½ cup extra-virgin olive oil

In a blender or small food processor, combine the parsley, garlic, vinegar, salt, and pepper. Pulse a few times. With the machine on, preferably set on low speed, gradually add the olive oil through the hole. Eventually the sauce will thicken. Stop to scrape down the sides of the blender jar, then blend briefly again on high speed.

MAKES ABOUT ⅔ CUP

A Tiny-Bit-Sweet Pan-Roasted Pot Roast

There's nothing better on a cold night than a hearty pot roast, chock-full of juicy meat and an assortment of tasty vegetables. The sweetness here, which comes from cinnamon, brown sugar, and raisins, makes this especially appealing to kids. The ultimate comfort food, this is even better when made ahead. You can cook it a couple of hours in advance and set it aside at room temperature for up to 2 hours or refrigerate it and serve it the next day. The flavor will only deepen.

2½ pounds beef chuck steak, in 1 piece
Salt and freshly ground pepper
2 tablespoons olive oil
2 cans (14½ ounces each) beef broth
1 can (14½ ounces) stewed tomatoes
6 garlic cloves, sliced
¼ cup raisins
2 tablespoons dark brown sugar
1 tablespoon ground cinnamon
6 carrots, peeled and cut into 2-inch pieces
6 small white boiling onions, peeled and halved
6 celery stalks, cut into 2-inch pieces
6 small red potatoes, scrubbed and halved
2 medium turnips, peeled and cut into thick slices
½ fresh fennel bulb, cored and thickly sliced (optional)

1. Trim any excess fat from the chuck. Pat dry. Season liberally with salt and pepper all over. Heat the olive oil in your nonstick frying pan over high heat. Add the meat and cook, turning, until nicely browned on both sides, about 4 minutes per side.

2. Add the broth, stewed tomatoes with their juices, garlic, raisins, brown sugar, and cinnamon. Stir to combine. Cover the pan, reduce the heat to low, and simmer for 1½ hours, turning the meat over after 45 minutes and basting occasionally with the pan juices.

3. Add the carrots, onions, celery, potatoes, turnips, and fennel to the pan and stir to coat with the liquid. If necessary, add enough water to the pan so that the liquid comes about halfway up the meat and vegetables. Cover again, raise the heat to medium-low, and cook, stirring the vegetables until they are tender, 20 to 30 minutes. Season with salt and pepper to taste. Remove from the heat and let stand, covered, for at least 15 minutes before serving.

SERVES 4 TO 6

PICADILLO WITH RAISINS, OLIVES, AND ALMONDS

Whether you interpret this as Cuban, Spanish, or Mexican, it's a dressed-up ground beef dish that can be served to kids as well as to company. Start with an avocado, orange, and grapefruit salad. Serve the picadillo with steamed white rice. To stretch the stew to feed six adults, add a side of black beans as well. This cooks up beautifully in the pan and tastes even better reheated.

3 tablespoons olive oil
I large onion, chopped
I green bell pepper, chopped
2 garlic cloves, minced
2 teaspoons ground cumin
I teaspoon dried oregano, preferably Mexican
¼ teaspoon crushed hot red pepper
I½ pounds lean ground round
I can (14½ ounces) diced tomatoes
I tablespoon balsamic vinegar
I bay leaf
I teaspoon salt
½ teaspoon freshly ground pepper
½ cup raisins
⅓ cup slivered almonds
⅓ cup sliced pimiento-stuffed olives
¼ cup medium-dry sherry

1. Heat the olive oil in your nonstick frying pan over medium-high heat. Add the onion and cook, stirring occasionally, until softened and just beginning to color, 3 to 5 minutes. Add the bell pepper and garlic and cook 2 minutes. Add the cumin, oregano, and hot pepper and cook, stirring, 1 minute longer.

2. Crumble the beef into the pan and cook, stirring to break it up into small pieces, until the meat loses its pink color. Add the tomatoes with their juices, the vinegar, bay leaf, salt, and pepper. Bring to a boil, reduce the heat to low, cover, and simmer 20 minutes.

3. Stir in the raisins, almonds, and olives. Simmer, uncovered, 10 minutes. Stir in the sherry and simmer 5 minutes longer. Before serving, remove and discard the bay leaf and season with additional salt and pepper to taste.

SERVES 4 TO 6

Veal Scaloppine with Lemon Vodka Sauce

There are entire countries that might not have their own cuisines if it weren't for the glorious lemon. In the following recipe, it's easy to figure out where the extra lemon flavor comes from. Serve with rice or orzo to soak up all the sauce.

1 cup flour
1 teaspoon salt
¼ teaspoon freshly ground pepper
1½ pounds veal scaloppine
3 tablespoons butter
2 tablespoons vegetable oil
2 garlic cloves, minced
1 cup reduced-sodium canned chicken broth
½ cup fresh lemon juice (from about 2 lemons)
¼ cup lemon-infused vodka, such as Absolut Citron
1 teaspoon sugar
Lemon slices, for garnish

1. In a pie plate, mix the flour with the salt and pepper. Dredge the veal scaloppine in the seasoned flour to coat; shake off any excess.

2. In your nonstick frying pan, melt 1½ tablespoons of the butter in half the oil over medium-high heat. Add the veal in batches without crowding and sauté, turning once, until lightly browned and just cooked through, 1 to 2 minutes per side. Remove to a plate. When the pan becomes dry, add the remaining butter and oil.

3. Add the garlic to the pan and cook just until softened and fragrant, about 1 minute. Add the broth, lemon juice, vodka, and sugar. Boil until the liquid is reduced by one-third, about 5 minutes.

4. Reduce the heat to low. Return the veal to the pan, cover, and simmer for a few minutes to reheat and blend the flavors. Arrange the veal on a platter. Pour the sauce over the meat, garnish with the lemon slices, and serve.

SERVES 4 TO 6

ROSEMARY VEAL CHOPS WITH QUICK PAN SAUCE

Since veal is pricey, it's automatically dinner party fare, although the minimal amount of work involved in this fragrant recipe makes it easy enough for a weekday supper. Sauté some sliced zucchini and garlic in olive oil, then toss it with spaghetti to serve on the side.

3 tablespoons olive oil
4 thick veal loin chops (about 2½ pounds total)
3 garlic cloves, sliced
1 tablespoon finely chopped fresh rosemary
¼ teaspoon crushed hot red pepper
⅔ cup reduced-sodium canned chicken broth
⅓ cup dry white wine
1 tablespoon minced lemon zest
Salt and freshly ground black pepper

1. Preheat the oven to 425 degrees F. In your nonstick frying pan, warm 1 tablespoon of the oil over medium-high heat. Pat the chops dry. Add them to the pan and cook, turning once, until browned, about 8 minutes. Transfer the chops to a shallow baking dish, set them in the oven, and bake until done to your liking, 15 to 20 minutes for pale pink and juicy. Remove from the oven and let rest for 5 minutes.

2. Shortly before the chops are done, pour off any oil but do not clean the pan. Set the pan over low heat. Add the remaining 2 tablespoons oil and when it is hot, add the garlic, rosemary, and hot pepper. Cook until the garlic is soft and just golden, 3 to 5 minutes.

3. Add the broth, wine, and lemon zest. Bring to a boil over high heat. Cook, stirring often and scraping the bottom of the pan until the sauce has thickened slightly and is becoming syrupy, about 3 minutes. Remove from the heat and season with salt and pepper to taste. Pour the sauce around and over the chops and serve immediately.

SERVES 4

Pan-Grilled Pork Chops with Almost-Instant Apricot Chutney

Quick, fresh chutneys are one of the hottest new trends in cooking. The mix of sweet, sour, and spicy piques the palate and perks up simple grilled and broiled meats with little effort. Here's a tantalizing combination that's as hearty as it is flavorful. Serve with rice or couscous.

4 center-cut pork chops, bone-in or boneless, trimmed of fat
2 teaspoons fresh lemon juice
½ teaspoon dried thyme leaves
½ teaspoon allspice
½ teaspoon hot paprika
½ teaspoon salt
¼ teaspoon freshly ground pepper
1 cup (about 4½ ounces) dried apricots
½ cup finely diced white onion
1 garlic clove, minced
1 to 2 jalapeño peppers, seeded and minced
2 tablespoons apricot preserves
2 tablespoons rice vinegar
1½ tablespoons vegetable oil

1. Trim any excess fat from the pork. In a small bowl, mix together the lemon juice, thyme, allspice, hot paprika, salt, and pepper. Rub this spice paste over both sides of the pork chops. Set them aside while you make the chutney.

2. Put the apricots in your nonstick frying pan and cover with cold water. Bring to a boil over high heat. Boil for 2 minutes, or until soft; drain. In a food processor, combine the softened apricots with the onion, garlic, 1 or 2 jalapeño peppers (depending on how hot you like your chutney), the apricot preserves,

and vinegar. Pulse until the apricots and onion are finely chopped. Season with a pinch of additional salt. Scrape the chutney into a serving bowl.

3. Rinse the pan and wipe dry. Add the oil and warm over medium-high heat until it shimmers. Add the chops and cook, turning, until they are lightly browned, about 3 minutes on each side. Pour ½ cup water into the pan, reduce the heat to medium-low, cover, and cook, turning once, until the chops are just cooked through with no trace of pink but still juicy, about 7 minutes. Serve the pork chops hot, with a dollop of chutney on the side.

SERVES 4

PORK, APPLES, AND PRUNES IN BOURBON CREAM SAUCE

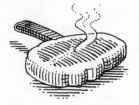

Even a 12-inch pan can get too overloaded to cook properly. It takes kitchen wisdom to sauté meat in several batches (thus browning it properly), rather than dumping it all in at once (which causes the meat to steam and become gray). The reward for this patience—richly browned pan drippings that provide the basis for an utterly addictive sauce—is worth it. Serve mashed potatoes and a plain green vegetable with this.

2 small pork tenderloins (about 1¾ pounds total), trimmed and cut into ¾-inch cubes

2 tablespoons corn oil

2 tablespoons butter

1 sweet red apple, cored and cut into ½-inch chunks

¼ cup finely chopped shallots

1 tablespoon flour

3 tablespoons bourbon

1 cup reduced-sodium canned chicken broth

⅓ cup heavy cream

½ cup quartered pitted prunes

¼ teaspoon salt

⅛ teaspoon freshly ground pepper

1. Pat the pork cubes thoroughly dry. Set your nonstick frying pan over medium-high heat. When it is hot, add the oil. Working in 2 batches, cook the pork cubes, turning them once, until browned on 2 sides, about 8 minutes total. Transfer the browned pork to a bowl; lower the heat if the pan gets too hot.

2. Pour off any oil remaining in the pan but do not clean the pan. Add the butter, set the pan over medium heat, and when the butter melts, add the apple. Cook, stirring once or twice, until browned, about 3 minutes. Add the shallots

and cook, stirring often, without browning, for 1 minute. Add the flour and cook, stirring often, for 1 minute.

3. Set the pan off the heat. Add the bourbon. Avert your face and ignite it with a match. Return the pan to low heat and shake it gently until the flames subside. Stir in the broth, cream, prunes, salt, and pepper. Bring to a simmer and cook, uncovered, stirring occasionally, until the sauce has thickened and the pork is just cooked through while remaining juicy, 5 to 7 minutes.

SERVES 4

Quick Skillet Choucroute

Without being sexist, I have to tell you that even though my wife loves this too, to me choucroute is guy food. That's because I think of it as beer and brats—only all in one pan and without the bun. Of course, you can add any fancy cured meats you like, but I find that a little fresh pork and smoked bratwurst or kielbasa make a terrific simple—and inexpensive—supper. In a pinch, just franks will do.

The cut of pork I use here is called "country ribs." These are actually meaty chops from the large end of the loin, cut in half down the center by the butcher. You end up with a compact piece of lean pork with a bone only at the short end. One of the prime advantages of using country ribs for skillet dishes is how easily they fit in the pan.

Since I assume that anyone who chooses choucroute likes sauerkraut, rinse it briefly to remove excess salt and brine, but don't soak it so much that the taste is lost. Serve with chewy rye bread and an assortment of mustards.

1 pound sauerkraut
1½ tablespoons olive oil
1 medium onion, thinly sliced
6 pork country ribs (about 1½ pounds)
Salt and freshly ground pepper
1 bottle or can (12 ounces) beer
1 tablespoon brown sugar
1 tablespoon Dijon mustard
2 bay leaves
½ teaspoon caraway seeds (optional)
3 links of bratwurst, cut in half, or ¾ pound smoked kielbasa, cut into
    2-inch lengths

1. Rinse the sauerkraut briefly under cold running water. Drain it well and squeeze dry.

2. Heat the oil in your nonstick frying pan over medium heat. Add the onion and cook, stirring occasionally, until it is soft and pale golden, 4 to 6 minutes.

3. Season the ribs all over lightly with salt and pepper. Push the onion to the side and add the ribs to the pan. Cook, turning, until the ribs are lightly browned all over, about 5 minutes.

4. Pour the beer into the pan. Mix in the brown sugar and mustard. Add the bay leaves and the caraway seeds, if you like them. Spoon the sauerkraut over all, stirring to mix it with the liquid in the pan. Cover and simmer over medium-low heat, stirring occasionally, 15 minutes.

5. Turn the ribs over, keeping them covered with sauerkraut. Tuck the pieces of bratwurst around the pan. Continue to simmer, covered, until most of the liquid is absorbed and the ribs are fully cooked through and tender, 20 to 25 minutes longer.

SERVES 6

Sausages and Peppers

What's so great about quick pan cooking is that you can whip up a tasty concoction like this in no time and use it in any number of different ways later on. This hearty mélange makes a great hero, grinder, or submarine filling—depending upon which part of the country you are from—or a terrific topping for pasta or polenta. Choose hot or sweet sausages according to your preference. Just remember, if you go to the trouble of getting really good sausages at an Italian butcher, the dish will taste that much better.

2 tablespoons extra-virgin olive oil
I large sweet onion, such as Vidalia, sliced
2 medium bell peppers, preferably I red and I green, sliced
I pound Italian sausages—pork, turkey, or chicken
I cup dry white wine
I tablespoon balsamic vinegar
½ teaspoon dried oregano
¼ to ½ teaspoon crushed hot red pepper
I cup tomato puree
Salt and freshly ground pepper

1. In your nonstick frying pan, heat the olive oil over high heat. Add the onion and cook, tossing, until golden and brown at the edges, about 5 minutes. (The trick is to cook the onion enough to bring out its sweetness and flavor.) Add the sliced bell peppers and cook, tossing, until they just soften, about 3 minutes. Scrape into a bowl.

2. Prick the sausages all over with the tip of a knife. Place in the pan with ¾ cup of the wine, cover, and bring to a boil. Cover, reduce the heat to medium, and cook, turning the sausages occasionally, until they are cooked through, the wine evaporates, and they brown nicely. Remove to a cutting board. As soon as the sausages are cool enough to handle, cut lengthwise in half and then crosswise into 1- to 2-inch pieces.

3. Pour the remaining ¼ cup wine and the vinegar into the skillet. Add the oregano and hot pepper and boil over high heat until the liquid is reduced by half. Pour the tomato puree into the pan, reduce the heat to medium, and simmer for 5 minutes.

4. Add the sausages, peppers, and onion to the sauce and simmer 5 minutes longer. Season with salt and pepper to taste.

SERVES 3 OR 4

COUNTRY SPARERIBS BRAISED WITH BACON AND BEER

For every quick little pan of eggs there's a long-simmered dish like this one. Either way, the pan is a man's best friend in the kitchen—have I made that clear by now? The gravy this dish produces is perfect over a batch of your best mashed potatoes.

3 pounds thick-cut (2 inches) pork loin country chops, halved crosswise
1½ tablespoons vegetable oil
4 slices of thick-cut bacon, coarsely chopped
1 large onion, finely chopped
2 large carrots, chopped
4 garlic cloves, chopped
½ teaspoon dried thyme leaves
1 bay leaf
2¾ cups reduced-sodium canned chicken broth
½ cup mellow dark beer, such as oatmeal stout
½ cup canned crushed tomatoes with puree
½ teaspoon salt
Freshly ground pepper
1½ tablespoons cornstarch

1. Pat the ribs dry. Set your nonstick frying pan over high heat. When it is hot, add the oil. Lay the ribs in the pan and cook, turning and rearranging occasionally, until well browned, about 10 minutes total. Transfer to a bowl. Pour off any fat from the pan but do not clean it.

2. Set the pan over medium heat. Add the bacon and cook, stirring occasionally, until it is beginning to brown, 3 to 5 minutes. Add the onion, carrots, garlic, thyme, and bay leaf. Cover and cook, stirring once or twice, for 10 minutes, or until the onion is golden.

3. Return the ribs to the pan. Add 2½ cups of the broth, the beer, tomatoes, salt, and a generous grinding of pepper. Cover and bring to a simmer. Cook, turning and rearranging the ribs to promote even cooking, until they are very tender, about 1 hour and 45 minutes.

4. Transfer the ribs to a platter and cover to keep warm. Strain the braising liquid, discarding the solids. Skim as much fat as possible off the liquid. Return the chops and the braising liquid to the pan, set over low heat, and slowly bring to a simmer.

5. In a small bowl, whisk the remaining ¼ cup broth into the cornstarch. Gradually stir the cornstarch mixture into the simmering liquid. Cook, turning the ribs and basting them with the liquid until they are heated through and the liquid has thickened into a gravy, about 5 minutes. Season with additional salt and pepper to taste before serving.

SERVES 4

LAMB CHOPS WITH PERNOD

Fifteen years ago I was served a leg of lamb that had been marinated in part with aniseed or fennel seed. It was the best piece of meat I had ever put in my mouth. For years I tried to re-create the slightly licoricey taste (and I otherwise *hate* licorice), but not even several pounds of anise at a time seemed to do the trick. That's how I came up with this Pernod-flavored recipe. Serve with oven-roasted rosemary potatoes and a tomato, mozzarella, and basil salad drizzled with a good olive oil.

Note: Canned beef broth is called for here because most people won't bother to make it from scratch. Nonetheless, it's actually almost as easy to make your own lamb and/or veal stock, which is what I use, as it is to open the cans and prepare them for recycling. (Just keep it simple: Combine several pounds of some veal and/or lamb bones with boiling water and a little salt and pepper and any carrots, celery, or onions you have lying around. Boil rapidly until the stock is reduced by one-third, 20 to 30 minutes.)

I tablespoon olive oil
½ tablespoon Dijon mustard
¼ teaspoon salt
¼ teaspoon freshly ground pepper
4 boneless loin lamb chops, cut about I inch thick
I cup beef broth
⅓ cup Pernod or other anise-flavored liqueur

1. Combine the olive oil, mustard, salt, and pepper in a bowl and stir to make a paste. Coat both sides of the lamb chops with the paste.

2. In your nonstick frying pan, cook the lamb chops over high heat until brown, 3 to 5 minutes. Turn the chops over and cook until the other side is browned and the chops are done to your liking, 3 to 5 minutes for rare to medium-rare.

3. Add the beef broth to the pan and boil until reduced by half. Add the Pernod and carefully ignite with a match. When the flames subside, remove the lamb chops to a serving dish, pour the sauce in the pan over the meat, and serve at once.

SERVES 4

LAMB CHOPS SAUTÉED WITH SWEET PEPPERS AND OLIVES

While you can make this sauté with chunks of boneless lamb cut from the leg, loin of lamb is so succulent and the meat cooked on the bone so flavorful that I like to do it with thinly cut loin chops. Be sure to ask the butcher to cut them specially for you, because prepackaged loin chops will be thicker than desired for this recipe.

6 loin lamb chops, cut ½ inch thick (about 1¼ pounds)
3 garlic cloves—2 thinly sliced, 1 crushed through a press
1 teaspoon dried rosemary
½ teaspoon salt
½ teaspoon coarsely cracked black pepper
2 tablespoons olive oil
1 small red onion, thinly sliced
1 small red bell pepper, cut into thin strips
½ cup dry white wine
1 tablespoon red wine vinegar
¼ cup pitted kalamata olives, thinly sliced
1 tablespoon unsalted butter

1. Trim any excess fat off the chops; there probably won't be much. Rub the crushed garlic over the meat and season with ½ teaspoon of the rosemary and the salt and pepper. Rub 1 tablespoon of the olive oil over the lamb. Let stand at room temperature for 30 to 60 minutes.

2. Heat the remaining 1 tablespoon olive oil in your nonstick frying pan over high heat. Add the lamb chops and sauté, turning once, until nicely browned outside but still pink in the center, about 2 minutes per side. Remove to a small platter and cover with foil to keep warm.

3. Add the red onion to the pan and sauté, stirring often, until softened, 2 to 3 minutes. Add the bell pepper and sliced garlic and sauté 2 minutes longer.

4. Pour the wine and vinegar into the pan. Add the remaining ½ teaspoon rosemary and the olives. Boil over high heat until the liquid is reduced by half, 1 to 2 minutes. Remove from the heat and stir in the butter until melted. Pour the contents of the pan over the lamb chops and serve at once.

SERVES 2 OR 3

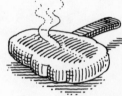

Glazed Ham Steaks with Raisin Sauce

Sizzled up in the pan, thick steaks of good ham are napped with a tangy raisin sauce, recalling Midwestern farmhouse abundance.

1 tablespoon peanut or canola oil
1 large or 4 individual thick ham steaks (about 1½ pounds total), patted dry
1 cup plus 1 tablespoon reduced-sodium canned chicken broth
1/3 cup dry red wine
1/3 cup dark or golden raisins
2 tablespoons red currant jelly
1 tablespoon whole-grain mustard
1/4 teaspoon freshly ground pepper
1 teaspoon cornstarch
1 tablespoon unsalted butter

1. Preheat the oven to 250 degrees F. In your nonstick frying pan, warm the oil over medium heat. Add the ham and cook, turning once, until browned, 8 to 10 minutes total. Transfer the ham to a plate and keep warm in the oven. Pour off any fat from the pan but do not clean it.

2. Set the pan over medium-low heat. Add 1 cup of the broth, the wine, and the raisins. Bring to a simmer and cook, uncovered, stirring occasionally and scraping the browned bits from the bottom of the pan, until the liquid has reduced slightly and the raisins are plump, 4 to 5 minutes.

3. Add the jelly, mustard, and pepper to the pan and continue to simmer, stirring often, until the jelly has melted. In a small bowl, whisk the remaining tablespoon of broth into the cornstarch and stir into the pan. Cook, stirring, until the sauce thickens, another 30 seconds or so. Whisk in the butter and remove from the heat.

4. Cut the ham into serving portions if necessary and transfer to plates. Spoon the sauce over the steaks and serve.

SERVES 4

CHAPTER 3

CHICKEN IN THE PAN

Japanese Fried Chicken

Faux Tandoori Chicken

Spanish Chicken Sauté with Olives and Almonds

Chicken 'n' Biscuits

Southern Cracker–Fried Chicken

"Chicken-Fried" Chicken with Pan Gravy

Voodoo Chicken

Chunky Chicken Liver Pâté with Marsala

Chicken Breasts in Madeira Mushroom Sauce

Chicken Chili with Corn, Peppers, and Black Beans

Chicken Saltimbocca

Chicken Piccata

Skillet Chicken Curry with Apples, Raisins, and Cashews

Chicken Breasts Stuffed with Spinach and Camembert

Smothered Chicken with African Flavors

Sticky Finger Hot Wings

Michael's Jerk Chicken Thighs with Banana Rum Relish

Turkey and Mushroom Paprikash

Japanese Fried Chicken

Many Japanese restaurants have some version of Asian Fried Chicken on their menus. For years I had tried to duplicate this dish without success. Finally I asked a Japanese chef for the secret. In so many polite words he told me, "Marinate it in soy sauce, you idiot." Actually, I subsequently discovered that I prefer teriyaki sauce because it's less salty, but the sentiment remains the same.

This recipe is so simple it's ridiculous, but as with all pan-fried chicken (excluding cutlets), you're going to have to cheat a bit. The problem is you want the oil very hot so the chicken will be crisp, which means it probably will be undercooked near the bone. The worry-free solution is to heat the chicken up first in a microwave. Since microwaves cook from the center out, they allow you to get rid of the pink in the center before the outside is flash-fried in the pan.

2 pounds chicken parts, such as wings, legs, and thighs (breasts only if bone
    is removed)
1 cup teriyaki sauce
½ cup flour, for dredging
Salt
1 teaspoon freshly ground pepper
½ cup canola or vegetable oil

1. Place the chicken in a shallow microwave-safe container. Pour the teriyaki sauce over the chicken. If you have time, marinate, turning once or twice, for about 30 minutes. Microwave on high for 3 minutes.

2. Combine the flour, salt, and pepper in a plastic container with a lid. Add the chicken, cover, and shake to coat thoroughly.

3. Heat the oil in your nonstick frying pan over high heat. Add the chicken pieces and cook, turning frequently, until brown and crisp, 8 to 10 minutes. Drain on paper towels.

SERVES 3 OR 4

Faux Tandoori Chicken

Real tandoori chicken is, of course, cooked in an Indian clay oven, or tandoor. The next best way to reproduce it is on the outdoor barbecue grill. But with this recipe, and using your skillet in the kitchen, you can still re-create a large part of that unique tandoori flavor. The secret is in the marinade.

The good news is that although the chicken is usually marinated overnight, since the marinade here doubles as a sauce, the actual standing time can be minimal.

1 frying chicken (about 3 pounds), cut up
1 teaspoon paprika
1 teaspoon salt
1 teaspoon freshly ground pepper
1 cup yogurt
2 tablespoons fresh lime juice
1 tablespoon grated fresh ginger
4 garlic cloves, crushed through a press
1 teaspoon ground cumin
¼ teaspoon cayenne
2 tablespoons vegetable oil

1. Make 2 deep gashes in each piece of chicken. Rub the chicken all over with the paprika, salt, and pepper.

2. In a large bowl, combine the yogurt with the lime juice, ginger, garlic, cumin, and cayenne. Mix well. Add the chicken and turn to coat. Marinate, turning the pieces several times, at least 1 hour at room temperature or overnight in the refrigerator.

3. Remove the chicken from the marinade and pat dry; reserve the marinade. In your nonstick frying pan, heat the oil over medium heat. Add the chicken and cook, turning once, until lightly browned all over, 5 to 7 minutes per side.

4. Pour the marinade over the chicken and bring to a simmer. Reduce the heat to medium-low, cover, and cook for 10 to 15 minutes, until the chicken is tender, with no trace of pink near the bone. Remove the chicken to a serving platter.

5. Skim any excess fat off the surface of the sauce. Simmer uncovered for several minutes to thicken slightly. Season with additional salt and pepper to taste. Pour over the chicken and serve.

SERVES 4

Spanish Chicken Sauté with Olives and Almonds

Spanish food, while lush with Mediterranean ingredients like tomatoes, garlic, olives, and almonds, is not as well known in this country as I think it should be. Here's a fabulous dish for entertaining, enlivened with a generous dose of sherry, that can be ready in less than half an hour. Serve with rice or couscous.

1 chicken (about 3 pounds), cut into 8 pieces
Salt, freshly ground pepper, and hot paprika
2 tablespoons olive oil, preferably extra-virgin
1 onion, chopped
2 garlic cloves, thinly sliced
⅓ cup sliced almonds
1 tablespoon tiny capers
⅔ cup medium-dry sherry
1½ tablespoons sherry wine vinegar or red wine vinegar
1 can (14½ ounces) diced tomatoes in juice
½ teaspoon sugar
1 jar (2½ ounces) Spanish pimiento-stuffed olives

1. Trim any fat from the chicken and season the pieces lightly with salt, pepper, and paprika.

2. Heat the olive oil in your nonstick frying pan over medium-high heat. Add the chicken, in 2 batches if necessary, and cook, turning, until browned, about 8 minutes. Remove to a plate. Pour off all but 2 tablespoons fat from the pan.

3. Add the onion, reduce the heat to medium, and cook, stirring occasionally, until it is soft and beginning to color. Add the garlic, almonds, and capers and cook, stirring, for 2 minutes longer.

4. Pour the sherry and vinegar into the pan and boil over high heat until the liquid is reduced by half. Add the diced tomatoes with their juice and the sugar.

5. Return the chicken to the pan and baste with the juices. Cover the pan, reduce the heat to medium-low, and cook, basting the chicken and turning occasionally, for 20 minutes.

6. Add the olives and continue to cook until the chicken is cooked through and tender, about 10 minutes longer.

SERVES 4

Chicken 'N' Biscuits

When you're looking for some cozy comfort food guaranteed to appeal to the entire family, here's a dish to choose. The chicken and gravy are cooked first; they can even be prepared a day or two in advance. Shortly before serving, the dumplings are baked in a hot oven. The chicken is served alongside, with the gravy ladled over the biscuits. Serve with peas and carrots or steamed broccoli.

1 chicken (about 3 pounds), cut up
Salt and freshly ground pepper
3 tablespoons olive oil
1½ tablespoons butter
1 medium onion, chopped
1 celery rib, chopped
2 tablespoons flour
3 cups homemade chicken stock or reduced-sodium canned chicken broth
½ teaspoon dried thyme leaves
1 bay leaf
3 tablespoons heavy cream
Buttermilk Drop Biscuits (recipe follows)

1. Trim any excess fat from the chicken. I like to remove most of the skin, too, because even browned first, it will end up soft after stewing and removing it makes a much leaner dish. Season the pieces generously with salt and pepper.

2. Heat 2 tablespoons of the olive oil in your nonstick frying pan over medium heat. Add the chicken and cook, turning, until lightly colored, about 5 minutes on each side. Remove to a plate and set aside. Pour off the drippings in the pan.

3. Add the butter and the remaining 1 tablespoon oil to the pan along with the onion and celery. Cook over medium heat, stirring occasionally, until soft but not brown, 3 to 5 minutes. Sprinkle the flour into the pan and cook, stirring,

1 to 2 minutes, without allowing it to color. Whisk in the chicken stock and bring to a boil, stirring until smooth and thickened. Add the thyme and bay leaf.

4. Return the chicken to the pan along with any juices that have collected on the plate. Cover the pan, reduce the heat to medium-low, and simmer, turning the pieces once or twice, until the chicken is so tender it's almost falling off the bone, about 1 hour. Skim off any fat you see on the surface of the sauce. Remove and discard the bay leaf. Stir in the cream and season with salt and pepper to taste.

5. The biscuits should be freshly baked. Either bake them just as the chicken is finishing, or make the chicken and gravy ahead and reheat it after you bake the biscuits. To serve, plate the pieces of chicken. Put a couple of biscuits alongside the chicken on everybody's plate and ladle the gravy over both the chicken and biscuits.

SERVES 4

Buttermilk Drop Biscuits

1½ cups sifted flour
1½ teaspoons baking powder
½ teaspoon baking soda
½ teaspoon salt
2 tablespoons butter
2 tablespoons solid white vegetable shortening
¾ cup plus 2 tablespoons buttermilk

Preheat the oven to 425 degrees F. Stir together the flour, baking powder, baking soda, and salt in a medium bowl. Cut in the butter and shortening until the mixture is the consistency of very coarse meal. Make a well in the center. Pour in the buttermilk and stir until it is just barely mixed. The secret of light biscuits is to handle the dough as little as possible. Using 2 ordinary tablespoons, scoop up a mound of dough and scrape it off onto a greased cookie sheet, allowing at least 2 inches between biscuits. Bake 12 to 15 minutes, until the biscuits are nicely browned.

MAKES ABOUT 16

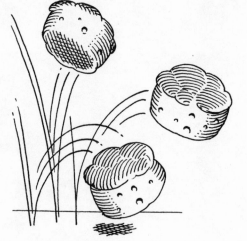

SOUTHERN CRACKER–FRIED CHICKEN

This is a variation of a recipe from a restaurateur friend of mine from my home-town of Memphis. (His version is for fried shrimp.) The pulverized crackers produce a lighter crust than flour, almost like tempura. To pulverize the crack-ers, I've recommended using a food processor to save time. But there is also something wonderfully tactile—and soothing—about crushing crackers by hand with a rolling pin.

3 pounds chicken drumsticks, thighs, or breasts
⅓ cup buttermilk
30 saltine crackers, pulverized in a food processor or by hand
I teaspoon rubbed sage
½ teaspoon garlic powder
½ teaspoon salt
I teaspoon freshly ground pepper
1½ cups canola or other vegetable oil

1. Place the chicken in a heatproof glass or ceramic bowl and cook in a mi-crowave oven on high for 4 minutes, turning once. (This is so you don't have to worry about the center of the chicken being undercooked.) Let the chicken cool slightly.

2. In the meantime, place the buttermilk in a shallow bowl. Combine the crushed crackers, sage, garlic powder, salt, and pepper in a plastic bag; shake to mix thoroughly. Dip the chicken pieces in the buttermilk. Place 1 or 2 pieces at a time in the bag and shake to coat.

3. In your nonstick frying pan, heat the oil over high heat until hot but not smoking. Add the chicken pieces and cook, turning frequently, until brown and crispy, about 20 minutes. Drain on paper towels before serving.

SERVES 4

"CHICKEN-FRIED" CHICKEN WITH PAN GRAVY

Here's how to get that Southern-fried chicken effect in your pan without the mess of the full-blown, deep-fried thing. Covered with a crunchy cracker coating and shallow-fried until crisp and brown, these chicken breasts are about as satisfying as it's possible for white meat to get. Spoon some of the gravy over the chicken and the rest over a mound of mashed potatoes, which make the ideal accompaniment.

4 large skinless, boneless chicken breasts (about 6 ounces each)
1 cup saltine cracker crumbs
¼ cup plus 2 tablespoons flour
Freshly ground pepper
1 egg
¼ cup buttermilk
¾ cup peanut oil
2½ cups milk
Salt

1. Trim any fat off the chicken breasts. Gently pound the thicker half of each piece to flatten evenly.

2. In a wide shallow bowl, mix together the cracker crumbs, ¼ cup flour, and ½ teaspoon of the pepper. In a second bowl, beat the egg slightly. Whisk in the buttermilk.

3. One at the time, dip a chicken breast into the egg mixture, then dredge in the cracker mixture to coat completely. Pat firmly to encourage the cracker crumbs to stick. Set the chicken on a plate.

pan, warm the oil over medium heat. When it is hot, the pan. Cook until well browned on the bottom, and cook, until nicely browned on the second side in the center, 4 to 5 minutes. Drain the chicken on a platter and cover with foil to keep warm.

ns of the cooking oil through a strainer into a bowl. dd the cracklings from the strainer to the pan. (The other batch of chicken.) Whisk the remaining 2 ta- nd cook, stirring often, and scraping the bottom of n, for 2 minutes. Gradually whisk in the milk. Stir poon pepper. Raise the heat slightly and simmer the dium thick, 3 to 5 minutes. Pour a little gravy over der in a sauceboat on the side.

Voodoo Chicken

I love recipes that call for a "secret ingredient," particularly one that gives the finished dish a slightly exotic flavor. Such is the case with this Voodoo Chicken. The secret ingredient here is ("and the envelope, please") . . . peanut butter! Even if you, like my wife, are not a big peanut butter fan, you will love the way this turns out. It is also a great dish to serve to guests if for no other reason than to watch them try to guess the secret ingredient. Serve over rice.

2 pounds skinless, boneless chicken breasts, cut into ½-inch strips
Salt and freshly ground pepper
2 tablespoons vegetable oil
2 large onions, chopped
2 red bell peppers, cut into thin strips
2 garlic cloves, finely chopped
I can (14½ ounces) chicken broth
¾ cup peanut butter
I teaspoon crushed hot red pepper
I package (10 ounces) frozen peas, thawed

1. Season the chicken with salt and pepper. In your nonstick frying pan, heat the oil over medium heat. Add the chicken strips and sauté, stirring often, for 3 minutes, or until the chicken turns opaque. Remove the chicken to a plate.

2. Add the onions, bell peppers, and garlic to the pan. Sauté 3 minutes, or until the onions are tender. Add the broth and peanut butter. Stir in the hot pepper. Simmer, stirring occasionally, for 10 minutes.

3. Stir in the chicken strips and peas. Cook 5 to 10 minutes, stirring occasionally, until the sauce is thickened and the dish is heated through.

SERVES 4

CHUNKY CHICKEN LIVER PÂTÉ WITH MARSALA

You will love this recipe even if, like myself, you aren't that fond of chicken livers. The Marsala adds just the right hint of sweetness. The mashing required is also a great way of getting rid of a little free-floating aggression.

8 strips of bacon
3 tablespoons butter
2 tablespoons olive oil
I pound chicken livers, trimmed
I medium onion, finely chopped
I garlic clove, minced
⅔ cup Marsala wine
I teaspoon salt
I teaspoon freshly ground pepper

1. In your nonstick frying pan, cook the bacon over medium heat until lightly browned and crisp, 4 to 5 minutes. Drain the bacon on paper towels, let cool, then crumble. Pour off all but 1 to 2 tablespoons of bacon fat from the pan.

2. Melt the butter in the olive oil in the pan over medium-high heat. Add the chicken livers, onion, and garlic. Cook, turning frequently, until the chicken livers are browned on the outside, 5 to 6 minutes.

3. Using the back of a fork, begin to mash and chop the chicken livers in the pan for 2 to 3 minutes. Add the Marsala, salt, pepper, and crumbled bacon and continue mashing and stirring until the Marsala is partially reduced and the chicken livers are at a desired doneness and consistency, anywhere from 2 to 5 minutes. Serve hot or cold over toast or with crackers (I prefer saltines). Covered and refrigerated, this pâté will last several days.

SERVES 6

Chicken Breasts in Madeira Mushroom Sauce

The combined flavors of nutty-sweet Madeira and woodsy wild mushrooms turn this quick chicken pan dish into fine bistro fare. Avoid stronger mushrooms, like porcini or shiitake, but seek out chanterelles or lobster mushrooms, which will lend the sauce their great-looking golden color. Heavy cream can stand in for tangy crème fraîche if need be, but add a few drops of lemon juice to balance the flavors just before serving.

¾ ounce dried wild mushrooms
1¼ cups reduced-sodium canned chicken broth
¼ cup medium-dry Madeira wine, such as Rainwater
4 large skinless, boneless chicken breast halves (about 6 ounces each)
2 tablespoons canola oil
3 tablespoons butter, softened
2 tablespoons minced shallot
1 garlic clove, minced
¼ teaspoon dried thyme leaves
Salt
½ cup crème fraîche or heavy cream
Pinch of freshly grated nutmeg
1 tablespoon flour
Freshly ground pepper

1. Rinse the mushrooms well in a strainer under cold running water. In a small saucepan, combine the broth and Madeira. Bring to a simmer. Add the mushrooms, cover, remove from the heat, and let stand, stirring once or twice, until cool.

2. With a slotted spoon, remove the mushrooms from the liquid. Let the liquid settle, then pour off and reserve the clear portion; discard the gritty residue. Mince the mushrooms.

3. Trim off any fat from the chicken. With a meat pounder or the bottom of a skillet, gently flatten the thicker end of each breast half. Pat dry.

4. In your nonstick frying pan, heat the oil over medium-high heat. When it is hot, add the chicken breasts to the pan and cook, rearranging them in the pan to promote even cooking and turning them once, until lightly browned on both sides, 6 to 8 minutes total (the chicken breasts will still be slightly pink at the center). Transfer to a plate.

5. Add 2 tablespoons of the butter to the pan and reduce the heat to low. Stir in the shallot, garlic, and thyme. Cook, stirring once or twice, 1 to 2 minutes, to soften. Add the minced mushrooms, cover, and cook, stirring once or twice, for 5 minutes. Stir in the reserved mushroom soaking liquid and ¼ teaspoon salt. Bring to a simmer and cook, partially covered, for 5 minutes.

6. Whisk the crème fraîche and nutmeg into the skillet. Add the chicken breasts. Partially cover the pan and simmer the breasts, turning them and basting them once or twice with the sauce, for 3 minutes. In a small bowl, mash together the remaining 1 tablespoon butter and the flour until smooth. Gradually whisk the flour mixture into the sauce. Season with pepper to taste. Continue to simmer, basting the breasts often, until they are just cooked through while remaining juicy and the sauce has thickened, 2 to 3 minutes.

SERVES 4

Chicken Chili with Corn, Peppers, and Black Beans

1 pound skinless, boneless chicken breasts
½ teaspoon salt
¼ teaspoon freshly ground pepper
2 strips of bacon, finely diced
1 medium onion, chopped
1 tablespoon olive oil
1 green bell pepper, cut into ½-inch dice
1 red bell pepper, cut into ½-inch dice
2 garlic cloves, minced
1½ tablespoons chili powder
1 teaspoon ground cumin
½ teaspoon dried oregano
1 can (14½ ounces) diced tomatoes
1 cup reduced-sodium canned chicken broth
1 can (15 ounces) black beans, rinsed and drained
1 can (11 ounces) corn kernels
Hot sauce

1. Trim any fat or gristle from the chicken. Cut the meat into ½-inch or smaller dice. Toss with the salt and pepper to season.

2. In your nonstick frying pan, cook the diced bacon and chopped onion in the olive oil over medium heat until the bacon renders most of its fat and the onion is softened, 3 to 4 minutes.

3. Add the bell peppers and garlic and cook, stirring, 2 minutes. Add the chicken and cook, tossing, until the chicken is no longer white, 2 to 3 minutes. Add the chili powder, cumin, and oregano and cook, stirring, 1 to 2 minutes, to toast the spices.

4. Add the tomatoes with their juice, the chicken broth, and the black beans. Bring to a boil, mashing some of the beans with the back of a large spoon. Reduce the heat to low, cover, and simmer until the chicken is just cooked through, about 5 minutes.

5. Mix in the corn and simmer 1 to 2 minutes longer. Season with additional salt, pepper, and hot sauce to taste.

SERVES 6

Chicken Saltimbocca

Italian food remains perennially popular, as does white meat chicken; so I figure any recipe that incorporates both is sure to be a winner. Add some nice color and speed of preparation, and you have a company dish that will win raves. Serve with buttered pasta tossed with coarsely cracked pepper and a little grated Parmesan cheese.

4 skinless, boneless chicken breasts (about 5 ounces each)
Salt and freshly ground pepper
1 tablespoon olive oil
½ lemon, cut into 2 wedges
2 teaspoons dried sage leaves
4 large paper-thin slices of prosciutto (about 1 ounce)
1 small shallot, minced
½ cup dry white wine
1 cup chicken broth
1 tablespoon unsalted butter

1. Trim any fat or gristle from the chicken breasts and pound them lightly to even thickness. Season lightly with salt and pepper.

2. Heat the olive oil in your nonstick frying pan over medium-high heat. Add the chicken breasts and cook, turning, until lightly browned outside but still pink in the center, 1½ to 2 minutes on each side. Remove the chicken to a plate and reduce the heat to medium-low.

3. Squeeze the juice from 1 lemon wedge over the chicken. Sprinkle half the sage leaves over the chicken, crumbling them coarsely, and cloak each chicken breast in a slice of prosciutto.

4. Add the shallot and remaining sage leaves to the pan and cook until the shallot is softened, 1 to 2 minutes. Pour in the wine and boil over high heat until reduced by half. Return the chicken to the pan and add the broth. Bring the liquid to a boil.

5. Reduce the heat to low, cover the pan, and cook, basting the chicken with the sauce, until the meat is cooked through and white throughout but still juicy; it will feel firm to the touch but still have a little give. Remove the chicken from the pan and boil the liquid until reduced to about ½ cup. Season with the juice of the other lemon wedge and additional pepper to taste; it probably won't need salt, because the prosciutto is salty. Remove from the heat and whisk in the butter just until melted. Pour over the chicken and serve.

SERVES 4

CHICKEN PICCATA

While this Italian classic is traditionally made with veal, baby beef is out of favor, and chicken cutlets, pounded until thin, make an excellent substitute. Lemon zest, the colored part of the peel, along with lemon juice, ensures a pleasingly tart, vibrant flavor. Serve with steamed broccoli or asparagus and a side of simple pasta or rice.

4 skinless, boneless chicken cutlets
Salt and freshly ground pepper
1 lemon
1½ tablespoons olive oil
1 garlic clove, cut in half
½ cup dry white wine
Dash of cayenne
1½ tablespoons chopped fresh parsley, preferably flat-leaf
Lemon slices and parsley sprigs, for garnish

1. With a chicken cutlet, the tenderloin is already removed, so there is a flat piece of skinless, boneless chicken breast. If you have breasts with the tenderloin attached, either remove and save it for another use or just fold it out. Gently pound the chicken between 2 sheets of waxed paper until they are an even ⅜ inch thick. Season lightly with salt and pepper.

2. With a zester, remove enough zest from the lemon to equal 1 teaspoon. Squeeze the juice from the entire lemon and strain out any seeds.

3. Heat the olive oil in your nonstick frying pan along with the garlic over medium-high heat. When the oil is hot and the garlic begins to brown, remove it and discard. Add the chicken breasts to the pan and sauté quickly, turning once, until lightly browned and just white throughout but still moist, 2 to 3 minutes on each side. Remove to a platter.

4. Pour in the wine and bring to a boil. Add the lemon zest and 2 tablespoons of the lemon juice. Taste and season with additional salt, the cayenne, and more lemon juice to taste. Stir in the parsley and pour the sauce over the chicken. Garnish with lemon slices and sprigs of parsley and serve at once.

SERVES 4

SKILLET CHICKEN CURRY WITH APPLES, RAISINS, AND CASHEWS

Trying to brown lots of little cubes of anything drives me crazy. Here, in a compromise that preserves my sanity, chicken breasts are browned first, which adds depth to the curry. Then they are diced to expose as much of their surface area as possible to the savory sauce during a final simmer. The fragrant, nutty rice called basmati is the curry's ideal companion.

4 large skinless, boneless chicken breast halves (about 6 ounces each)
3 tablespoons peanut oil
1 medium onion, halved and thinly sliced
1 small sweet apple, cored, peeled, and diced
2 tablespoons minced fresh ginger
3 garlic cloves, minced
2 tablespoons plus 1 teaspoon curry powder, preferably Madras
¼ teaspoon cayenne
1 tablespoon plus 1 teaspoon flour
1 can (14½ ounces) reduced-sodium chicken broth
3 plum tomatoes, seeded and chopped
½ cup well-stirred canned unsweetened coconut milk
⅓ cup raisins
1 teaspoon salt
¾ cup frozen tiny peas, thawed
Hot steamed rice, preferably basmati, as accompaniment
Chopped cashews and mango chutney

1. Trim off any fat from the chicken breasts. Gently pound each breast to an even thickness. Pat dry.

2. In your nonstick frying pan, heat 1 tablespoon of the oil over medium heat. When the oil is hot, add the chicken breasts and cook, turning once, until lightly

browned on both sides, about 8 minutes total. (The chicken will still be slightly pink in the center.) Transfer to a cutting board.

3. Add the remaining 2 tablespoons oil to the pan and reduce the heat to medium-low. Stir in the onion, apple, ginger, garlic, curry powder, and cayenne. Cover and cook, stirring occasionally and scraping the bottom of the pan, for 5 minutes. Sprinkle on the flour and cook, uncovered, stirring often, for 2 minutes. Gradually stir in the broth. Add the tomatoes, coconut milk, raisins, and salt. Bring to a boil, stirring until the sauce thickens. Reduce the heat to medium-low, partially cover, and simmer for 10 minutes.

4. Meanwhile, cut the chicken into ¾-inch cubes. Add the chicken cubes to the pan and simmer, uncovered, stirring occasionally, for 7 minutes. Add the peas and cook until the chicken is just white in the center but still juicy, about 3 minutes longer. Serve over hot rice. Pass chopped cashews and mango chutney in separate bowls and let everyone help themselves.

SERVES 4

CHICKEN BREASTS STUFFED WITH SPINACH AND CAMEMBERT

If your market carries bags of prewashed and trimmed fresh spinach, by all means use it. It will cut the prep time in half. As a substitute, you can use frozen chopped spinach, as long as you thaw it first and squeeze firmly to remove as much moisture as possible. Camembert contributes a unique flavor here, but feta is also extremely compatible. Use whichever you have on hand.

2 tablespoons extra-virgin olive oil
1 pound fresh spinach leaves, preferably prewashed baby spinach
1 garlic clove, minced
⅛ teaspoon freshly grated nutmeg
Salt and freshly ground pepper
4 ounces cold Camembert cheese, rind removed, finely diced, or ½ cup
**   crumbled feta cheese**
4 skinless, boneless chicken breast halves (about 6 ounces each)
⅓ cup flour
¾ cup dry white wine
1 tablespoon unsalted butter

1. In your nonstick frying pan, heat 1 tablespoon of the olive oil over medium-high heat. Gradually add the spinach to the pan, stirring as it wilts, until it all fits in nicely. Add the garlic and cook, stirring, until the spinach is just tender, about 1 minute. Remove to a colander and press to remove as much liquid as possible. Transfer to a cutting board and coarsely chop. Put the spinach in a bowl. Season with the nutmeg and a pinch each of salt and pepper. Stir in the cheese.

2. With a sharp knife, cut a pocket horizontally across the middle of each chicken breast, trying not to cut all the way through. Stuff each piece of chicken with one-fourth of the spinach filling. Skewer the edges with wooden toothpicks to seal.

3. Mix the flour with ¼ teaspoon salt and ⅛ teaspoon pepper. Roll the stuffed chicken breasts in the seasoned flour to coat. Shake off any excess.

4. Wipe out the skillet, then heat the remaining 1 tablespoon olive oil in the pan over medium-high heat. Add the stuffed chicken breasts and cook, turning, until lightly browned on both sides, 6 to 8 minutes total. Pour the wine into the pan. Reduce the heat to medium-low, cover, and cook, turning the chicken once, until it is white throughout with no trace of pink, about 10 minutes.

5. Remove the chicken breasts to plates. Boil the liquid in the pan over high heat until reduced to about ⅓ cup, 2 to 3 minutes. Whisk in the butter, pour the sauce over the chicken, and serve at once.

SERVES 4

SMOTHERED CHICKEN WITH AFRICAN FLAVORS

This is a healthy colorful recipe that is great fun serving to guests. It also makes a cozy Sunday supper and even though the flavors are exotic kids will love it.

Don't be turned off by the number of ingredients; it's actually a very simple dish to make. I prefer to make it several hours ahead of time, then reheat it just before serving.

2 tablespoons olive oil
8 chicken thighs, skin removed and preferably deboned
Salt and freshly ground pepper
1 medium onion, chopped
1 tablespoon minced garlic
1 tablespoon ground cumin
1 tablespoon ground cinnamon
1 teaspoon ground coriander
1 teaspoon paprika
1 tablespoon minced fresh ginger
1 can (14½ ounces) reduced-sodium chicken broth
1 medium sweet potato, peeled and cut into bite-size chunks
2 tablespoons fresh lemon juice
½ cup coarsely chopped dried apricots
½ cup dark raisins
½ cup sliced almonds

1. In your nonstick frying pan, heat the olive oil over medium-high heat until hot but not smoking. Add the chicken thighs and brown well (in 2 batches if your sauté pan is not large enough), 3 to 4 minutes per side. Season the chicken thighs with salt and pepper to taste.

2. Add the onion to the pan, reduce the heat to medium, and cook, stirring often, until the onion begins to brown, 5 to 7 minutes. Add the garlic and cook, stirring frequently, 1 minute. Add the cumin, cinnamon, coriander, paprika, and ginger. Cook, still stirring frequently, for 1 minute longer. Add the broth, sweet potato, lemon juice, dried apricots, raisins, and almonds. Return the chicken thighs to the pan and bring the mixture just to a boil. Stir so that the chicken is on the bottom.

3. Reduce the heat to low, cover, and cook until the chicken thighs are tender, 35 to 45 minutes. If the sauce becomes too thick, thin with a little additional broth or water. Season with salt and pepper to taste before serving.

SERVES 4

STICKY FINGERS HOT WINGS

These wings are addictive and so easy to make in a 12-inch nonstick skillet, you'll find yourself whipping up a batch on the spur of the moment both for the kids and for company. The seasoned wings fried up through step 2 can be served plain or dipped, Buffalo wing–style, in blue cheese dressing. Finished in the sticky hot sauce suggested here, though, I've found them irresistible crowd pleasers. If you want to make a double recipe, fry them up in two batches, then finish them off all together in the sauce. One caution: Jam gets very hot, so don't let any little fingers reach for these until they've had a few minutes to cool off.

2¾ pounds good-sized chicken wings (12 to 14)
1½ teaspoons salt
1 teaspoon hot paprika
1 teaspoon dried thyme leaves
½ teaspoon ground cumin
½ teaspoon freshly ground pepper
¼ cup vegetable oil
½ cup apricot jam
1½ tablespoons Dijon mustard
1½ tablespoons cider vinegar
1 teaspoon your favorite hot pepper sauce, or to taste
1 garlic clove, crushed through a press

1. Cut the wing tips off the chicken wings and reserve them for stock or just discard. Pat the chicken dry. Cut the two larger wing joints in half and place them in a large bowl. In a small bowl, mix the salt, hot paprika, thyme, cumin, and pepper. Sprinkle over the chicken and toss to coat evenly.

2. In your nonstick frying pan, heat the oil over medium-high heat for about 1 minute until hot. Add the wings. You may have to squeeze them a bit, but they will fit in a single layer. Cover the pan and reduce the heat to medium-low. Cook

for 7 minutes, or until the wings are golden brown on the bottom. Turn over and cook 7 minutes. Turn again to color any pale spots and continue to cook, covered, 7 to 8 minutes longer, until the wings are a deep golden brown and moist inside but with no trace of pink. Remove with tongs and drain on paper towels. Pour the oil out of the pan. Carefully wipe out the pan with paper towels.

3. You don't need to strain the apricot jam, but if it has large chunks of fruit, chop them up. Place the apricot jam in a small bowl. Add the mustard, vinegar, hot sauce, and garlic and whisk until well blended. Scrape the sauce into the pan. Bring to a boil, reduce the heat to medium, and cook for about 1 minute to remove the raw garlic taste.

4. Add the chicken to the pan and cook, turning, until the sauce has thickened and the wings are evenly glazed, about 2 minutes. Serve hot, warm, or at room temperature.

SERVES 4 TO 6 AS AN APPETIZER

MICHAEL'S JERK CHICKEN THIGHS WITH BANANA RUM RELISH

Fiery jerk chicken is always going to taste best when you're eating barefoot on a beach in Jamaica. Second best, however, is aspiring chef, Michael Kassar's stovetop version, which he learned from his Jamaican-raised mom. Serve lots of fluffy white rice and drink Jamaican Red Stripe beer.

½ cup thinly sliced scallions
1 to 2 jalapeño peppers, stemmed and chopped
3 garlic cloves, peeled and chopped
1½ tablespoons minced fresh ginger
1 tablespoon packed light brown sugar
1 tablespoon soy sauce
1 tablespoon fresh lime juice
1 tablespoon rum
1 tablespoon Pickapeppa Sauce (or another steak sauce)
½ teaspoon ground allspice
¼ teaspoon dried thyme leaves
1¾ pounds skinless, boneless chicken thighs, trimmed of any excess fat
2 tablespoons olive oil
½ cup chicken broth
Banana Rum Relish (recipe follows)

1. In a blender or food processor, combine the scallions, jalapeño, garlic, ginger, brown sugar, soy sauce, lime juice, rum, Pickapeppa Sauce, allspice, thyme, and 1 tablespoon water. Blend the sauce until smooth.

2. In a medium bowl, toss the chicken with the sauce. Cover and marinate at room temperature, stirring once or twice, for 1 hour.

3. In your nonstick frying pan, heat the olive oil over medium heat. Add the chicken pieces, reserving any marinade in the dish. Cook on one side, rearranging the chicken pieces to promote even cooking, until lightly browned, about 6 minutes. Turn over and cook until just cooked through but still moist in the center, about 5 minutes. Transfer the chicken to plates.

4. Add the broth and reserved marinade to the pan and bring to a boil over high heat. Cook, stirring and scraping up the browned bits from the bottom of the pan, until the sauce is reduced by half, 2 to 3 minutes. Spoon the sauce over the chicken and serve, passing the banana relish at the table.

SERVES 4

Banana Rum Relish

2 tablespoons raisins

2 tablespoons rum

1 medium-ripe but firm banana, diced

1 medium plum tomato, seeded and diced

1 tablespoon finely diced red onion

½ jalapeño pepper, stemmed and minced

1 teaspoon fresh lime juice

¼ teaspoon salt

1. In a medium bowl, combine the raisins and rum. Let stand, stirring occasionally, until the raisins have softened somewhat, about 1 hour.

2. Add the banana, tomato, red onion, jalapeño, lime juice, and salt. Stir to combine. Let stand for 15 minutes before using.

MAKES ABOUT 1 ½ CUPS

TURKEY AND MUSHROOM PAPRIKASH

2½ tablespoons olive oil

12 ounces large white mushrooms, quartered

1½ tablespoons butter

1 medium onion, chopped

2½ pounds boneless turkey thighs, cut into 2-inch chunks

2½ tablespoons sweet Hungarian paprika

1 tablespoon flour

½ cup dry white wine

1 can (14½ ounces) reduced-sodium chicken broth

½ ounce imported dried mushrooms

1 teaspoon dried thyme leaves

¼ to ½ teaspoon cayenne

⅔ cup sour cream

1. In your nonstick frying pan, heat half the olive oil over medium-high heat. Add the fresh mushrooms and sauté, tossing, until lightly browned, about 5 minutes. Remove to a bowl and set aside.

2. In the hot pan, melt the butter in the remaining 1¼ tablespoons oil over medium heat. Add the onion and cook until softened, 3 to 5 minutes. Add the turkey and cook, stirring occasionally, until lightly browned, 5 to 7 minutes.

3. Sprinkle the paprika and flour over the turkey. Cook, stirring, 1 to 2 minutes. Pour in the wine and bring to a boil, stirring to incorporate the flour and paprika. Add the broth, dried mushrooms, thyme, and cayenne. Bring to a boil. Reduce the heat to medium-low and cook, partially covered, 45 minutes.

4. Return the mushrooms to the pan and simmer 5 minutes longer. Remove from the heat, stir in the sour cream, and serve.

SERVES 4 TO 6

CHAPTER 4
SEAFOOD
IN THE PAN

Asian-Flavored Arctic Char

Corn-Crusted Catfish with Cajun Tartar Sauce

Red Snapper in White Wine with Tomatoes and Capers

Mustard-Glazed Salmon Steaks

Pan-Fried Trout with Lemon Butter, Capers, and Almonds

Spice-Crusted Fresh Tuna on Arugula

Fresh Tuna Burgers with Sesame-Ginger Mayonnaise

Shrimp au Poivre

Spaghetti with Fresh Clam Sauce

Crab Cakes with Mustard-Caper Sauce

Triple Ginger Pan-Barbecued Shrimp

Oyster Pan Roast

Pan-Steamed Mussels

ASIAN-FLAVORED ARCTIC CHAR

Arctic char is a delicate pink fish, related to salmon but leaner and milder. I find it very good eating and adaptable to a variety of seasonings. Other fish fillets that can be used in this recipe include salmon, snapper, bass, or even scrod.

2 garlic cloves
1 inch of ginger, cut into thin slices
2 teaspoons wasabi powder
3 tablespoons soy sauce
3½ tablespoons peanut oil
1½ tablespoons fresh lemon juice
1 teaspoon Asian sesame oil
2 Arctic char fish fillets, about 1 pound each
2 tablespoons butter
1 scallion, minced

1. Squeeze the garlic cloves through a press into a small bowl. Put the ginger slices, several at a time, into the press and squeeze as much juice as you can into the bowl. Whisk in the wasabi powder, soy sauce, 1½ tablespoons peanut oil, the lemon juice, and sesame oil.

2. Place the fish fillets, skin side down, in a pie plate or oval gratin just large enough to hold them in a single layer. Spoon half the wasabi sauce over the fish. Let marinate at room temperature for 15 to 20 minutes.

3. In your nonstick frying pan, melt the butter in the remaining 2 tablespoons peanut oil over medium-high heat. Add the fish, flesh side down, and cook for 2 minutes. Using a wide spatula, carefully turn the fillets over. Sauté, skin side down, for about 3 minutes, to crisp the skin slightly.

4. Pour ¼ cup water into the pan. Spoon the remaining sauce over the fish fillets and sprinkle the scallion evenly over the top. Cover the pan and cook 2 to 3 minutes longer, until the fish just flakes and is barely opaque in the center.

SERVES 4

Corn-Crusted Catfish with Cajun Tartar Sauce

This fish is not blackened (at least not on purpose), only pan-fried to a crisp and golden turn. A light crust of seasoned cornmeal produces this attractive effect, while a fiery tartar sauce supplies luscious heat. To complete the meal, serve Buttermilk-Scallion Hush Puppies (page 206) and your favorite coleslaw.

3 thick catfish fillets (about 2 pounds total)*
Salt and freshly ground pepper
¾ cup yellow cornmeal
I teaspoon cayenne
I teaspoon ground cumin
½ teaspoon dried thyme leaves, crumbled
¼ cup peanut or corn oil
Cajun Tartar Sauce (recipe follows)

1. Season the catfish fillets lightly but evenly on both sides with salt and pepper. In a pie plate, stir together the cornmeal, cayenne, cumin, and thyme.

2. In your nonstick frying pan, warm the oil over medium heat. Dredge the fillets in the seasoned cornmeal and transfer them to the pan. Cook, carefully turning once with a large spatula, until the crust is crisp and golden and the fish is just cooked through but still moist, about 10 minutes total.

3. Carefully cut each fillet crosswise into thirds and serve immediately. Pass the tartar sauce at the table.

*The pan will only hold 3 fillets, so buy thick ones, which can then be divided among 4 diners. Or just cook for 3, and serve each guest a whole fillet of regular thickness. This fish is so good, no one will ever claim you have given them too much.

SERVES 4

Cajun Tartar Sauce

The sauce tastes best when prepared a day or so before using.

¾ cup mayonnaise
1 tablespoon drained small (nonpareil) capers
1 tablespoon drained chopped pimiento
1 tablespoon minced dill pickles
1 tablespoon finely chopped onion
1 teaspoon hot pepper sauce, such as Tabasco
1 teaspoon Dijon mustard
¼ teaspoon Worcestershire sauce

In a small bowl, stir together all the ingredients. Cover and refrigerate overnight before using, if you have the time.

MAKES ABOUT 1 CUP

RED SNAPPER IN WHITE WINE WITH TOMATOES AND CAPERS

Red snapper takes well to seasoning, and this colorful sauce is special enough for company. The fish cooks in a flash, so if you have all your other ingredients prepped and ready to go, you can finish this off in little more than five minutes. Striped bass or cod would work equally well here. I am partial to mashed potatoes with fish, something you see in all the trendiest restaurants now, so that is what I serve with it.

1½ to 2 pounds red snapper fillets, about ½ inch thick
¼ cup flour
½ teaspoon salt
¼ teaspoon freshly ground pepper
3 tablespoons extra-virgin olive oil
1 large shallot, minced
2 garlic cloves, minced
2 plum tomatoes, seeded and diced
⅔ cup dry white wine
2 tablespoons diced (oil-packed) sun-dried tomatoes
1½ tablespoons tiny (nonpareil) capers
1½ tablespoons chopped fresh parsley

1. Cut the snapper into 4 equal pieces. Mix the flour, salt, and pepper. Dredge the fish pieces in the seasoned flour. Shake off any excess.

2. Heat your nonstick frying pan over medium-high heat for 1 minute. Add 2 tablespoons of the olive oil and heat for another minute. Add the fish, cover the pan, and cook for 2 minutes, until the bottom is golden brown. Turn the fish over, cover again, and cook for 2 minutes longer, or until the second side is browned and the fish is just cooked through. Remove the fish to a plate. Let the pan cool off the heat for a minute or two.

3. Add the last tablespoon of olive oil to the pan. Add the shallot and garlic and set over medium-low heat. Cook, stirring, until softened, about 1 minute. Add the plum tomatoes and cook for 1 minute longer. Pour in the wine. Add the sun-dried tomatoes, capers, and half the parsley. Boil until the liquid is reduced by about one-third, 1 to 2 minutes.

4. Return the fish to the pan and spoon the sauce up over it. Cover and simmer over low heat for 1 minute to heat through. Sprinkle on the remaining parsley. Transfer the fish to plates. Season the sauce with additional salt and pepper to taste. Spoon over the fish and serve at once.

SERVES 4

MUSTARD-GLAZED SALMON STEAKS

It's easy to show off with fish, and since it cooks so quickly, it makes a great choice for last-minute entertaining. Here a simple mustard sauce complements the meatiness of salmon. Boiled new potatoes and steamed asparagus are classic accompaniments. If you're drinking wine, pour a nicely chilled California Chardonnay.

**4 salmon steaks, cut 1 inch thick (6 to 8 ounces each)
Salt and freshly ground pepper
1 tablespoon butter
1 tablespoon olive oil
½ cup dry white wine
1½ tablespoons Dijon mustard
⅓ cup heavy cream
2 teaspoons fresh lemon juice**

1. Pat the salmon steaks dry with paper towels. Season on both sides with salt and pepper.

2. In your nonstick frying pan, melt the butter in the oil over medium-high heat. Add the salmon and sauté until lightly browned on the bottom, about 2 minutes. Using a wide spatula, carefully turn the steaks over and sauté until lightly browned on the second side, 1 to 2 minutes longer. Put the lid over the pan and carefully pour out as much of the oil as you can.

3. Pour the wine into the pan and boil until reduced by half, 1 to 2 minutes. Turn the salmon over one more time. In a small bowl, whisk the mustard into the cream. Blend in the lemon juice. Stir into the liquid in the pan.

4. Reduce the heat to medium-low. Cover and cook, spooning the mustard cream up over the fish once or twice, until the salmon is barely opaque in the center, 5 to 7 minutes. Transfer the salmon steaks to a small platter or plates. Season the sauce with salt and pepper to taste. Spoon over the fish and serve at once.

SERVES 4

Pan-Fried Trout with Lemon Butter, Capers, and Almonds

Long before supermarkets spruced up their fish departments, back when there were only frozen fish sticks and nondescript-looking fillets, about the only fresh fish you could buy was farm-raised trout. Maybe because there are so many other choices now, it's easy to forget just what good eating this delicate fish provides. Here's my favorite quick pan recipe for trout.

2 fresh trout, cleaned (head on or off to your taste)
Salt and freshly ground pepper
1½ tablespoons olive oil
2 tablespoons butter
2 tablespoons slivered almonds
½ cup dry white wine
2 tablespoons fresh lemon juice
2 teaspoons capers
½ teaspoon sugar

1. Pat the trout dry. Season them nicely inside and out with salt and pepper.

2. Add the olive oil to your nonstick frying pan and set it over high heat until almost smoking. Reduce the heat to medium-high and put the fish in the pan. Cover and fry for 3 to 4 minutes, until the bottom of the fish is browned. Loosen carefully with a wide spatula and turn the fish over. Cook the trout, still covered, until the second side is browned and the fish is cooked through near the bone. Remove the trout to a platter or 2 plates.

3. Add the butter to the pan. As soon as it melts, reduce the heat to medium and add the almonds. Cook, stirring, until lightly browned, about 30 seconds. Pour in the wine and bring to a boil, scraping up any brown bits from the bottom of the pan. Add the lemon juice, capers, and sugar. Boil until the liquid is reduced by at least half, 2 to 3 minutes. Pour the sauce and almonds over the trout and serve at once.

SERVES 2

SPICE-CRUSTED FRESH TUNA ON ARUGULA

What you're going for here is a firm crust on the outside, sashimi on the inside. Rick Becker, the recipe's creator, actually serves this as a Christmas dish because of its colors and the fact that it always gets so many ooohs and aaahs! from the seasonal crowd.

The recipe is pristine and simple. For a little extra flavor, and some pyrotechnics, after removing the tuna from the pan, add a mixture of a little fish or chicken stock, a tablespoon of mustard, and juice from one or two of the lemon wedges. Then add a splash of Cognac, flame, and boil until the sauce is reduced to the consistency of a thick salad dressing. Pour over the tuna and arugula and serve at once.

2 bunches arugula
3 tablespoons crushed coriander seeds
3 tablespoons freshly ground pepper
1 (2-pound) tuna steak, cut at least 3 inches thick
3 egg whites, lightly beaten
3 tablespoons safflower oil
2 lemons, cut into wedges

1. Thoroughly wash the arugula, remove any tough stems, and pat dry. Place in a large bowl and refrigerate.

2. Mix together the coriander seeds and pepper and spread over a cutting board or plate. Dip both sides of the tuna steak into the egg whites, then press the tuna into the pepper-coriander mixture, coating both sides well to form a crust.

3. Add the oil to your nonstick frying pan and set over high heat until the pan is very hot and the oil is beginning to smoke. Add the tuna and sear, turning once, until a crust is formed, about 3 minutes on each side. The fish will still be rare on the inside.

4. Remove the tuna from the pan, thinly slice, and spread over the arugula. Garnish with the lemon wedges.

SERVES 4

Fresh Tuna Burgers with Sesame-Ginger Mayonnaise

Skillet-seared and still just a little pink in the center, these hearty burgers of juicy fresh tuna manage to be every bit as rib-sticking as the beef kind. A ginger-spiked mayonnaise is the terrific complement—both exotic and richly comforting. Make some coleslaw and open your favorite Asian beer.

1 pound well-trimmed fresh tuna, chilled
⅓ cup plus 2 tablespoons mayonnaise
2 scallions, thinly sliced
¾ teaspoon grated fresh ginger
½ teaspoon soy sauce
¼ teaspoon Asian sesame oil
2 teaspoons peanut or canola oil
Salt and freshly ground pepper
2 large premium hamburger buns or sandwich rolls
12 or so large leaves of flat spinach, stemmed
2 thin slices from a large tomato

1. Cut the tuna into 1-inch cubes. In a food processor, pulse the chilled tuna to chop. (Do not puree; some texture, like that of ground beef, should remain.) Transfer to a bowl and stir in 2 tablespoons of the mayonnaise. Shape the tuna into 2¾-inch-thick patties about 5 inches in diameter. Cover and refrigerate if not cooking immediately.

2. In a small bowl, stir together the remaining ⅓ cup mayonnaise, the scallions, ginger, soy sauce, and sesame oil. Cover the sesame-ginger mayonnaise and refrigerate until using.

3. In your nonstick frying pan, warm the peanut oil over medium-high heat. When it is hot, add the patties to the pan. Cook until well browned, about 4 minutes. Turn over, season to taste with salt and pepper, and cook until done to your liking, another 4 minutes for pink-in-the-middle tuna.

4. Meanwhile, toast the buns if desired. Set the tuna burgers on the bun bottoms. Top each burger with half the sesame-ginger mayonnaise, then with the spinach leaves and tomato slices. Set the bun tops in place and serve immediately.

MAKES 2 SANDWICHES

SHRIMP AU POIVRE

To peel or not to peel? When pan-cooking shrimp, that is the question. If peeled, they cook—and are eaten—too quickly and do not fully absorb flavors. If unpeeled, all the flavors remain in the shells. My solution? Use half-peeled shrimp.

Insert the blade of a pair of kitchen scissors under the top shell and cut all the way to the tail. Remove the first segment or two of shell from each shrimp, leaving the tail end intact.

½ cup Cognac or good brandy
1½ pounds large shrimp, half-peeled (see above)
¼ cup olive oil
Juice from 1 lemon
2 teaspoons coarsely ground pepper
Salt
1 tablespoon Worcestershire sauce
1 cup heavy cream
Chopped parsley or chives for a little color

1. Pour half of the Cognac into a brandy snifter and sip occasionally while cooking your shrimp.

2. In a large bowl, combine the shrimp, olive oil, lemon juice, pepper, and ⅛ teaspoon salt. Toss to coat thoroughly. Allow to stand for at least 15 minutes.

3. Heat your nonstick frying pan over high heat. Sprinkle a few grains of salt into the pan. When the salt turns brown, add the shrimp with its marinade to the pan. Cook the shrimp, turning once, 3 to 4 minutes, until they are pink and curled.

4. Add the Worcestershire sauce to the pan and let sizzle for a few seconds. Add the Cognac and carefully ignite with a match. As soon as the flames subside, use a slotted spoon to remove the shrimp to a serving dish. Pour the heavy cream into the pan and boil over high heat, stirring frequently, until the sauce reduces by about one-third and thickens slightly, about 3 minutes. Season with salt to taste and pour over the shrimp. Garnish with parsley or chives and serve at once.

SERVES 4

SPAGHETTI WITH FRESH CLAM SAUCE

**SEAFOOD
IN THE PAN**

114

When you're in the mood for a great dinner quick and you have access to some really fresh clams, this is an amazingly easy dish that is perfect made in the pan. (The pasta, of course, is boiled on the side.) In authentic Italian fashion, there is just enough intensely flavored sauce to coat the pasta, not to drown it in. Serve an antipasto salad to start and pass garlic bread throughout, and don't forget to pour a well-chilled dry white wine, such as Soave, Pinot Grigio, or Sauvignon Blanc.

18 fresh littleneck clams
½ pound thin spaghetti or linguine
¼ cup extra-virgin olive oil
3 garlic cloves, thinly sliced, then cut into slivers
¼ teaspoon crushed hot red pepper
2 tablespoons chopped parsley
¼ teaspoon dried winter savory
¼ teapsoon dried thyme leaves (if you don't have savory, use ½ teaspoon dried thyme leaves)

1. Scrub the outside of the clams with a vegetable brush under cold running water to clean them. Put them in a bowl of cold water and soak for 10 minutes. Drain and rinse the clams. Fill the bowl with clean water and soak for another 10 minutes.

2. In a large pot of boiling salted water, cook the spaghetti until just barely tender, 9 to 10 minutes. Scoop out and reserve 1 cup of the pasta cooking water. Drain the spaghetti into a colander.

3. In your nonstick frying pan, warm the olive oil over medium heat. Add the garlic and cook until it just begins to color, 1 to 2 minutes. Add the hot pepper, 1 tablespoon of the parsley, the savory, and the thyme. Pour in ½ cup of the reserved pasta cooking water.

4. Arrange the clams in the pan in a single layer. Cover the pan and raise the heat to medium-high. Cook, turning the clams over once, until they open, 4 to 6 minutes. As soon as they open (and some will open before others), use tongs to remove the clams, letting any juices drip back into the pan. Discard any clams that do not open.

5. Quickly remove the clams from their shells. On a cutting board with a lip, quarter the clams or chop them coarsely. Return the clams to the pan along with any juices that have collected on the cutting board. Add the spaghetti and the remaining parsley to the pan and cook, tossing to mix with the clams and sauce, until just warmed through. If the sauce is too dry, add a little more of the pasta water. Serve at once.

SERVES 2 OR 3

CRAB CAKES WITH MUSTARD-CAPER SAUCE

Crab cakes as good or better than you get in trendy restaurants are not hard to make at home in the pan. To duplicate professional quality, though, you do have to spring for fresh lump crabmeat, which can be a bit pricey. I think you'll find these crisp cakes, with their sophisticated little sauce, well worth every penny. A simple rice pilaf and some steamed fresh asparagus turn this into the kind of meal a good restaurant gets twenty bucks for.

2 eggs
¼ cup mayonnaise
¾ teaspoon Tabasco sauce
I pound blue or Dungeness crabmeat, preferably jumbo lump, picked over
for bits of shell
⅓ cup fine, fresh bread crumbs, preferably from sourdough bread
¾ cup heavy cream
I tablespoon Dijon mustard
I tablespoon drained small (nonpareil) capers
Salt
I tablespoon butter
I tablespoon canola oil

1. In a large bowl, whisk together the eggs, mayonnaise, and ½ teaspoon of the Tabasco. In a strainer set over a medium bowl, press the crabmeat to extract any juices; reserve the juices. Add the crab and bread crumbs to the bowl and stir well. Cover and refrigerate for at least 1 hour.

2. In a heavy medium saucepan over medium heat, combine the cream and the crab juices from the bowl. Bring to a boil and cook, uncovered, stirring occasionally, until reduced to ⅔ cup, 6 to 8 minutes. Whisk in the mustard, capers,

and the remaining ¼ teaspoon Tabasco. Season with salt to taste. Remove from the heat and cover to keep warm.

3. Form the chilled crab mixture into four 4-inch cakes. In your nonstick frying pan, melt together the butter in the oil over medium heat. Carefully slide the crab cakes into the pan. Cover and sauté until light brown on the bottom, 3 to 4 minutes. Carefully turn over, cover again, and cook until lightly browned on the second side and cooked through.

4. Quickly reheat the sauce. To serve, set a crab cake on each of 4 heated plates. Spoon the sauce around the crab cakes and serve at once.

SERVES 4

Triple Ginger Pan-Barbecued Shrimp

Packed with irresistible sweet-hot East-West flavor, these shrimp can serve four to six people as a hot main course with rice and a vegetable or up to eight on toothpicks as an appetizer, in which case they are good warm, at room temperature, or even slightly chilled.

1½ pounds jumbo shrimp, shelled and deveined, preferably with tails intact
1½ tablespoons fresh lime or lemon juice
1 tablespoon ketchup
2 teaspoons soy sauce
1½ teaspoons Asian sesame oil
1 teaspoon honey
1 teaspoon grated fresh ginger
½ teaspoon powdered ginger
½ teaspoon curry powder
¼ teaspoon cayenne
1½ tablespoons vegetable oil
1½ tablespoons minced preserved ginger

1. In a medium bowl, toss the shrimp with the lime juice, ketchup, soy sauce, ¾ teaspoon of the sesame oil, the honey, fresh ginger, powdered ginger, curry powder, and cayenne. Let stand 15 to 30 minutes.

2. Heat the vegetable oil in your nonstick frying pan over medium-high heat. Add the shrimp with their marinade and sauté, tossing, until they are pink and lightly curled, about 3 minutes.

3. Remove from the heat and toss with the preserved ginger and the remaining ¾ teaspoon sesame oil. Serve hot, at room temperature, or slightly chilled.

SERVES 4 TO 6

OYSTER PAN ROAST

Here's manly food if there ever was any. An oyster pan roast is an oyster stew, but lighter because it's made with milk or half-and-half instead of heavy cream. The only trick is in finding fresh oysters. If they are already shucked, be sure to include all the liquor, or juices, for flavor. Garnish with chopped parsley, serve with tiny oyster crackers, and pass lemon wedges and a bottle of hot sauce on the side. This will serve two as a main dish, four as a starter.

2 tablespoons unsalted butter
I large shallot, minced
2 cups half-and-half or milk
I½ cups clam juice (bottled or canned)
¼ to ½ teaspoon hot paprika
2 dozen oysters, shucked, with liquor reserved, or I pint shucked oysters
Salt and freshly ground pepper

1. Melt the butter in your nonstick frying pan over medium heat. Add the shallot and cook, stirring, until soft but not brown, 2 to 3 minutes.

2. Pour the half-and-half and clam juice into the pan. Add the paprika and heat until steaming but not boiling.

3. Add the oysters with their liquor, or juices, and cook just until the edges curl and the oysters are plump and just firm but still tender. Season with salt and pepper to taste and serve at once.

SERVES 2 TO 4

PAN-STEAMED MUSSELS

A domed lid will help greatly here. If you don't have one or if your skillet is too shallow, make the liquid base, cook half the mussels, remove them with a skimmer or slotted spoon, then cook the remaining mussels in the same liquid. Mussels are high in protein and extremely low in fat. They're also inexpensive and quick-cooking. Be sure to set the table with soup spoons as well as forks, so diners can enjoy the delicious base once they've polished off the mussels. Chunks of crusty bread will help sop up the liquid, too. Drink cold beer or a well-chilled Sauvignon Blanc.

2 pounds fresh mussels, preferably farm-raised
1½ tablespoons olive oil
1 large shallot, chopped
Dash of crushed hot red pepper
1 cup dry white wine
2 tablespoons chopped fresh parsley

1. Rinse the mussels well under cold running water; I like to scrub them with a vegetable brush. Pull on the hairy brown "beard" of each to stretch it away from the shell and trim it off with a sharp paring knife.

2. In your nonstick frying pan, heat the oil over medium heat. Add the shallot and cook until it begins to soften, 1 to 2 minutes. Add the hot pepper and sizzle for about 10 seconds. Add the wine and half the parsley. Bring to a boil over high heat.

3. Add the mussels, cover, and steam, stirring them once to bring the bottom mussels to the top and the top mussels to the bottom of the pan, until the shells open, about 5 minutes. Remove the mussels as soon as they open with a skimmer or large spotted spoon and mound them in a large shallow serving bowl. If they continue to cook, they will toughen. Leave any mussels that don't open in

the covered pan for an extra couple of minutes. If the shells still don't open, discard them.

4. Strain the cooking juices in the pan through a sieve lined with a double thickness of dampened cheesecloth. This is important to remove any grit. Pour the hot liquid over the mussels, sprinkle with the remaining 1 tablespoon parsley, and serve at once.

SERVES 2 AS A MAIN COURSE, 4 AS A STARTER

CHAPTER 5

ONE-PAN MEALS

Garlicky Beans and Greens

Skillet Chicken Pot Pie with Artichokes and Mixed
   Vegetables

Skillet Chicken Ziti with Olives and Provolone

Chicken Fajitas
   Guacamole

Salmon-Orzo Pilaf

Creamy Fettuccine with Ham, Mushrooms, and Peas

Duck Fried Rice

Pork and Beans with Spanish Rice

Shrimp and Sausage Skillet Jambalaya

Chicken Livers and Dirty Rice

Asparagus, Vidalia Onion, and Mushroom Risotto

Dr. Roland's Midnight Rice RX:
   Curried Rice
   Mexican Black Beans and Rice
   Citrus Shrimp and Rice

Cincinnati Chili

Five-Alarm Trail Drive Chili

Vegetable Chili with Bulgur, Brown Rice, and Beans

Peppers Stuffed with Beef and Rice

Skillet Stuffed Cabbage

Meatball and Carrot Ragout

White Pan Pizza

Double-Crusted Turkey Sausage Pan Pizzas

Garlicky Beans and Greens

Everyone's eating less meat these days, at least part of the time. Here's a healthful high-fiber recipe that's full of punch. Toss it with pasta as suggested here for a lively vegetarian main course. Or skip the last step and serve the beans and greens as a side dish along with roast chicken or pork.

1 pound kale
3 tablespoons fruity extra-virgin olive oil
6 garlic cloves, thinly sliced, then cut into slivers
¼ teaspoon crushed hot red pepper or more to taste
1 can (14½ ounces) reduced-sodium chicken broth
Salt and freshly ground pepper
1 can (15 ounces) cannellini or Great Northern white beans, rinsed and
    drained
½ pound linguine, cooked and drained
Freshly grated Parmesan cheese (optional)

1. Rinse the kale well. Remove the tough stems. Stack the leaves and cut them into fine shreds. There should be 6 cups very tightly packed.

2. In your nonstick frying pan, heat the oil over medium heat. Add the garlic and cook 1 to 2 minutes, until just barely beginning to color. Sprinkle the hot pepper into the pan. Gradually add the shredded kale, stirring and turning it with 2 wooden spoons or with salad tongs to fit it all into the pan. Pour in the chicken broth, cover, and cook, stirring occasionally, until the kale is tender, 12 to 15 minutes. Season with salt and pepper to taste.

3. Stir the beans into the greens and simmer uncovered 2 to 3 minutes, stirring occasionally. Pour over the hot linguine and serve at once. Pass a bowl of grated cheese on the side.

SERVES 4

Skillet Chicken Pot Pie with Artichokes and Mixed Vegetables

For busy weekday nights, here's a no-brainer that's sure to please the kids. I take several of my favorite convenience foods, including a jar of marinated artichoke hearts, Bisquick, and that reliable standby, cream of chicken soup, and whip them up into a delectable meal in a pan in barely over half an hour. For the "etc." of the title, use your favorite frozen vegetable medley. When I can find it, I like to use corn, asparagus, and chopped red pepper. The mix adds great color as well as taste.

1 tablespoon olive oil
1 pound skinless, boneless chicken breasts, cut into 1-inch cubes
2 cups frozen vegetable medley (preferably corn, asparagus, and chopped red bell pepper)
1 jar (6 ounces) marinated artichoke hearts, drained and quartered
1 can (10 ounces) cream of chicken soup
1 egg
½ cup half-and-half
1 cup prepared baking mix, such as Bisquick

1. Heat the olive oil in your nonstick frying pan over medium-high heat. Add the chicken and toss until lightly browned outside, 3 to 4 minutes. Add the frozen vegetables and cook, stirring often, until they are thawed and crisp-tender, 2 to 3 minutes. Stir in the artichokes and undiluted soup. Bring to a simmer.

2. In a medium bowl, beat the egg lightly. Whisk in the half-and-half. Add the baking mix and stir just until incorporated. Do not overmix; small lumps are fine. Pour the batter over the chicken and vegetables in the pan.

3. Reduce the heat to low, cover, and cook until the top is lightly colored and baked through, about 35 minutes. Serve the pot pie right from the pan, scooping it up with a large spoon and making sure everyone gets a piece of crust along with some chicken and vegetables. As an alternative, you can invert the pot pie onto a deep platter, so that the colorful vegetables are on top.

SERVES 4

Skillet Chicken Ziti with Olives and Provolone

This hearty pan supper doesn't supply the same crusty edges and bottom that a baked ziti casserole would, but you won't have a fossilized baking dish to clean either. The eating is just as hearty and satisfying, however, and I think the trade-off is worth it. Sweet Italian sausage can be substituted for some or all of the chicken, if desired; just extend the browning time slightly.

**4 large skinless, boneless chicken breasts (about 6 ounces each), trimmed
    of any fat**
2 tablespoons olive oil
1 red bell pepper, cut into ¾-inch pieces
**½ pound brown (cremini) or fresh white mushrooms, trimmed and
    quartered**
Salt
3 garlic cloves, finely chopped
¼ teaspoon crushed hot red pepper
⅓ cup dry red wine
2¼ cups tomato sauce, preferably homemade
½ pound ziti
½ cup pitted kalamata olives
6 ounces sliced or shredded processed provolone cheese
Freshly grated Parmesan cheese

1. Pound the thicker ends of the chicken breasts gently to flatten evenly. Pat the chicken dry.

2. In your nonstick pan, warm 1 tablespoon of the oil over medium heat. Add the chicken breasts to the pan and cook, turning once, until lightly browned on both sides, about 8 minutes total (the chicken breasts will still be

slightly pink at the center). Transfer to a cutting board and let cool, then cut into ¾-inch cubes.

3. Set the pan over medium heat and add the remaining 1 tablespoon of oil. Add the red bell pepper and cook, stirring occasionally, until slightly softened, about 3 minutes. Add the mushrooms and a pinch of salt, cover, and cook, stirring once or twice, until the mushrooms begin to give up their juices, about 5 minutes. Uncover, stir in the garlic and hot pepper, and cook for 1 to 2 minutes, until the garlic is fragrant but not browned. Add the wine and bring to a boil. Cook, uncovered, stirring often, until the wine is reduced by half, about 2 minutes. Stir in the tomato sauce.

4. Meanwhile, bring a large pot of water to a boil. Add the ziti and 1 tablespoon salt. Cook according to the package directions, stirring occasionally, until just barely tender, 9 to 10 minutes; drain.

5. Stir the chicken, pasta, and olives into the sauce in the pan. Arrange the provolone cheese over the chicken mixture, cover, reduce the heat to medium-low, and simmer until the chicken is white in the center and the cheese is melted and gooey, about 5 minutes. Serve at once. Pass a bowl of grated Parmesan cheese on the side.

SERVES 4

Chicken Fajitas

Fajitas are traditionally grilled outdoors, but they taste just as good—maybe even better—when winter sets in and you turn to your pan for indoor assistance. Along with the usual fajita filling of marinated chicken, onion, and peppers, I've included a simple guacamole. If you prefer, you can skip it and just add a dollop of sour cream.

1¾ **pounds skinless, boneless chicken breasts**
3 **tablespoons soy sauce**
3 **tablespoons Worcestershire sauce**
1 **tablespoon balsamic vinegar**
1 **tablespoon dark brown sugar**
4 **garlic cloves, crushed through a press**
2 **serrano chiles, thinly sliced**
¼ **teaspoon liquid hickory smoke flavoring**
2 **tablespoons olive oil**
1 **medium onion, sliced**
2 **bell peppers, preferably red, thinly sliced**
3 **long green Anaheim chiles, thinly sliced**
¼ **teaspoon salt**
Guacamole (recipe follows) and spicy salsa, as accompaniments
8 **warm flour tortillas,* about 7 inches in diameter**

1. Trim any fat or gristle from the chicken. Gently pound the thicker ends to flatten evenly. In a shallow nonreactive dish, stir together the soy sauce, Worcestershire, vinegar, brown sugar, garlic, serrano chiles, and smoke flavoring. Add the chicken breasts and turn to coat. Cover and marinate at room temperature, turning several times, for 1 hour.

2. Heat 1 tablespoon of the olive oil in your nonstick frying pan over medium-high heat. Remove the chicken breasts from the marinade, reserving the

marinade, and add them to the pan. Cook, turning once, until well browned on both sides and cooked through but still juicy in the center, about 8 minutes in all. Transfer the chicken to a cutting board and set aside to cool for about 5 minutes.

3. While the chicken is cooling, strain the marinade; reserve the liquid and the serrano chiles separately. Rinse and dry the pan. Set it over medium-high heat and add the remaining 1 tablespoon oil. When it is hot, add the onion, bell peppers, and Anaheim chiles. Season with salt. Sauté for 5 minutes.

4. Quickly cut the chicken breasts lengthwise into ½-inch-wide strips. Stir the serrano chiles and 1 tablespoon of the reserved marinade liquid into the pan. Arrange the chicken over the vegetables. Cover and cook, shaking the skillet occasionally, until the vegetables are browned but still crunchy and the chicken is heated through, about 3 minutes.

5. To serve, set the pan of chicken and vegetables on a trivet right on the table. Set out bowls of the guacamole and salsa. Pass the warm tortillas in a covered basket and let diners assemble their own faijitas.

* Flour tortillas can be warmed in a microwave, as directed on the package, or wrapped in foil in two stacks in a 325 degree F oven for 5 to 10 minutes.

SERVES 4

Guacamole

While I've made the cilantro optional here, because sometimes it's hard to find, it gives the dish a distinctly Mexican taste. Nonetheless, guacamole without cilantro is infinitely better than no guacamole at all.

2 large ripe avocados, preferably Hass
2 to 3 teaspoons fresh lime juice
½ teaspoon salt
¼ cup finely chopped fresh cilantro (optional)

Cut the avocados in half. Remove the pits and scoop out the meat into a bowl. Mash with a fork until fairly smooth. Stir in 2 teaspoons of the lime juice, the salt, and the cilantro, if you have it. Taste and add the remaining 1 teaspoon lime juice if you think it needs it.

MAKES ABOUT 1¼ CUPS

This neat one-pan meal requires very little fuss. The salmon's rich flavor blends well with the bland affability of the rice-shaped pasta called orzo, which is perfect as a vehicle for the sauce.

2 tablespoons extra-virgin olive oil
I medium leek (white part only), rinsed well and chopped
I medium red bell pepper, chopped
¾ pound salmon fillet, skinned and cut into bite-size chunks
I½ cups orzo
3 cups chicken broth
½ cup heavy cream
2 tablespoons capers, drained
Salt and freshly ground pepper

1. Heat the olive oil in your nonstick pan over medium-high heat. Add the leek and red bell pepper. Cook, stirring, until the pepper just begins to soften, about 3 minutes. Add the salmon and cook, turning, until the fish cubes turn opaque on the outside, 2 to 3 minutes.

2. Add the orzo and cook, stirring, for 1 minute to coat it with the oil. Pour in the chicken broth. Bring to a boil, reduce the heat to low, cover, and cook until the pasta is tender, 10 to 12 minutes.

3. Stir in the cream and capers. Season with the salt and pepper to taste. Simmer until hot, about 1 minute, and serve at once.

SERVES 3 OR 4

CREAMY FETTUCCINE WITH HAM, MUSHROOMS, AND PEAS

Related to the dish known as pasta Alfredo, this traditional Italian formula adds smoky ham, woodsy mushrooms, and sweet peas to the mix, making the creamy sauce wonderfully flavorful, and colorful, too. Real imported Parmigiano-Reggiano is a must here. Choose a pasta shape, such as shells or orrechiette (little ears), that will capture the various small, bumpy elements of the sauce.

2 tablespoons unsalted butter
¼ pound lean smoky ham, diced
¾ pound imported semolina pasta, such as shells
Salt
½ pound brown (cremini) or fresh white mushrooms, trimmed and chopped
¼ teaspoon crushed hot red pepper
I cup heavy cream
Pinch of freshly grated nutmeg
I cup frozen tiny peas, thawed and drained
I cup freshly grated Parmesan cheese, plus more for serving
Freshly ground black pepper

1. In your nonstick frying pan, melt the butter over medium-low heat. Add the ham and cook, stirring occasionally, until just lightly browned, about 8 minutes. With a slotted spoon, transfer the ham to a bowl and reserve. Do not clean the pan.

2. Meanwhile, bring a very large pot of water to a boil. Add the pasta and 1 tablespoon salt and cook according to the package directions until almost tender, about 10 minutes.

3. While the pasta cooks, return the pan to medium heat. Add the mushrooms and ½ teaspoon salt. Cover and cook, stirring once or twice, until the mushrooms render their juices, about 5 minutes. Stir in the hot pepper and cook, stirring often, until the liquid evaporates and the mushrooms begin to brown, about 5 minutes. Return the ham to the pan. Stir in the cream and nutmeg and bring to a simmer.

4. At the last minute, stir the peas into the pot with the pasta. Drain immediately, shaking off as much water as possible, and transfer to the skillet. Stir in the 1 cup Parmesan cheese and cook, tossing and stirring often, until the sauce has thickened slightly and the pasta is tender, 3 to 5 minutes. Season generously with black pepper. Pass a bowl of grated cheese at the table.

SERVES 4 AS A MAIN COURSE, 6 AS A STARTER

DUCK FRIED RICE

Duck Fried Rice, as served at the China Grill of New York and Miami Beach, is unlike any other fried rice I've ever tasted. Not only is it deliciously satisfying, it is also quite filling—one portion can be a meal in itself.

Recently I realized that one of the key ingredients was not an ingredient at all but the consistency of the texture—a confetti of vegetables is finely chopped to approximate the size of grains of rice. With a tip of the hat to the China Grill, this is my version of this simple but sumptuous dish.

1 medium red bell pepper, coarsely chopped
2 broccoli stems, coarsely chopped
1 large carrot, peeled and coarsely chopped
6 scallions, coarsely chopped
6 large mushrooms, coarsely chopped
½ inch fresh ginger, peeled and chopped
1 tablespoon vegetable or canola oil
1 package (10 ounces) frozen peas
½ Chinese Roast Duck,* bones removed, coarsely chopped
½ cup slivered almonds (optional)
3 cups cold cooked rice
2 tablespoons good soy sauce
2 tablespoons mirin (Japanese sweet rice wine)

1. Combine the red bell pepper, broccoli, carrot, scallions, mushrooms, and ginger in a food processor and finely chop but do not pulverize.

2. In your pan, heat the oil over high heat until almost smoking. Add the mixture from the food processor and sauté for 4 to 5 minutes, stirring constantly, until the vegetables are tender.

3. Add the peas, duck, and almonds and cook for 3 minutes, stirring constantly. Add the rice, combine thoroughly, and cook, stirring constantly, until heated through, about 3 minutes.

4. Sprinkle the soy sauce and mirin over the rice. Toss thoroughly and cook for another 2 to 3 minutes. Serve immediately.

*Chinese roast duck adds fabulous flavor to this easy dish. If it is not available near you, substitute ½ pound Chinese roast pork from a take-out restaurant. Or cook up ½ pound bacon and chop it up.

SERVES 4

PORK AND BEANS WITH SPANISH RICE

ONE-PAN
MEALS

138

Here's my pan-prepared twist on pork and beans, done with a Latin-inspired hand. Dramatic black beans, cumin, and jalapeño peppers elevate the dish to a whole new level. In place of fatback or bacon, I use that tender "other white meat," lean pork loin. And the Spanish-flavored rice makes this a complete, hearty meal in a single pan.

2 tablespoons extra-virgin olive oil

I small pork tenderloin (about 12 ounces), cut into ½-inch cubes

I small onion, sliced

I large garlic clove, crushed through a press

I cup long-grain white rice

I can (14½ ounces) reduced-sodium chicken broth

I½ cups canned plum tomatoes, broken up with a fork

I to 2 tablespoons minced fresh jalapeño peppers, to taste

I teaspoon ground cumin

½ teaspoon salt

¼ teaspoon freshly ground black pepper

I can (16 ounces) pinto beans, rinsed and drained

1. Heat 1 tablespoon of the olive oil in your nonstick frying pan over medium-high heat. Add the pork cubes and cook, tossing and stirring, until the meat loses its pink color, 3 to 5 minutes. Remove to a bowl.

2. Heat the remaining 1 tablespoon oil in the same pan. Add the onion and garlic and cook, stirring occasionally, until softened, 3 to 4 minutes. Add the rice and cook, stirring, for 1 minute. Return the meat to the pan.

3. Add the chicken broth, tomatoes with their juices, jalapeño peppers, cumin, salt, and black pepper. Bring to a boil. Reduce the heat to low, cover, and cook until the pork is tender and most of the liquid is absorbed, 18 to 20 minutes.

4. Stir in the pinto beans and simmer for a few minutes to heat through.

SERVES 4

Shrimp and Sausage Skillet Jambalaya

Good times seem to follow automatically when Cajun and Creole foods are on the menu. Jambalaya may be the most festive of all such parties-in-a-dish, even when it's a quick weekday version simmered up in the pan. The spicy sausage called andouille is the first choice here, but pork or beef hot links from the supermarket work well, too.

2 tablespoons olive oil
6 ounces andouille sausage, diced
1 large red bell pepper, diced
1 cup finely chopped onion
½ cup finely chopped celery
4 garlic cloves, minced
1 teaspoon dried thyme leaves
1 teaspoon freshly ground black pepper
½ teaspoon ground cumin
½ teaspoon rubbed sage
⅛ teaspoon cayenne
2⅓ cups reduced-sodium canned chicken broth
1 cup long-grain white rice (not converted)
¾ cup canned crushed tomatoes with puree
¾ teaspoon salt
¾ pound medium shrimp, shelled and deveined
3 scallions, thinly sliced

1. In your nonstick frying pan, warm the oil over medium heat. Add the andouille and cook, stirring occasionally, until lightly browned, 8 to 10 minutes. With a slotted spoon, remove the andouille from the pan and reserve.

2. Return the pan to medium heat. Add the bell pepper, onion, celery, garlic, thyme, black pepper, cumin, sage, and cayenne. Cover and cook, stirring once or twice, until the vegetables are fairly tender, about 10 minutes. Stir in the chicken broth, rice, tomatoes, and salt. Bring to a simmer. Cover, reduce the heat to low, and cook for 15 minutes.

3. Stir in the andouille, cover, and cook for 5 minutes. Arrange the shrimp in a single layer over the rice. Cover and continue to cook until all the liquid has been absorbed and the rice is tender, 3 to 5 minutes longer. Stir the scallions into the rice, mixing the shrimp as you do so, remove the pan from the heat, and let stand, covered, for 5 minutes. Serve hot.

SERVES 4 TO 6

CHICKEN LIVERS AND DIRTY RICE

Not everyone likes chicken livers, but if you do, this is a really nice way to enjoy them. The large nonstick pan provides the ideal surface area for the initial sauté and the follow-up steeping in stock and vinegar keeps the livers moist and flavorful. This Southern dish is traditionally made with giblets as well as livers, but I simplified it a bit. When you see the color of the finished dish, you'll understand where it got its name. I usually toss a handful of chopped parsley over the top before I dish it out.

2 tablespoons olive oil
I large onion, sliced
I garlic clove, minced
4 ounces fresh white mushrooms, coarsely chopped
I pound chicken livers, trimmed and quartered
½ teaspoon dried thyme leaves
½ teaspoon salt
½ teaspoon freshly ground pepper
I cup long-grain white rice
2 cups beef broth
¼ cup red wine vinegar

1. In your nonstick frying pan, heat 1 tablespoon of the olive oil over medium-high heat. Add the onion and garlic and cook until they begin to turn golden around the edges, 4 to 5 minutes. Add the mushrooms and cook until they give up their juices, 3 to 5 minutes. Scrape into a bowl.

2. Heat the remaining 1 tablespoon oil in the same pan (no need to rinse) over medium-high heat. Add the chicken livers and season with the thyme, salt, and pepper. Sauté, tossing, until brown on the outside but still pink inside, about 3 minutes.

3. Return the onions, garlic, and mushrooms to the pan. Stir in the rice. Pour the broth and vinegar into the pan. Bring to a boil, reduce the heat to low, cover, and cook until the rice is tender and most of the liquid is absorbed, about 20 minutes.

SERVES 4

ASPARAGUS, VIDALIA ONION, AND MUSHROOM RISOTTO

Risotto is a natural for the pan. With its nonstick surface, there's no worry about sticking, and the large surface area speeds cooking time. Just be sure to adjust the heat to your particular pan so that the liquid bubbles slowly enough that the rice has a chance to absorb it before it evaporates.

I love risotto, and while it can serve as a first course, in place of pasta, to my mind, preceded by a tomato and mozzarella salad, it makes a perfect meal unto itself. This all-vegetable version is perfect for springtime.

1 medium portobello or 10 ounces fresh white mushrooms
¼ pound asparagus
2 tablespoons extra-virgin olive oil
1 medium Vidalia or other sweet onion, finely chopped
1½ cups Arborio rice
½ cup dry white wine
2 cans (14½ ounces each) reduced-sodium chicken broth
2 tablespoons butter
½ cup freshly grated Parmesan cheese
Salt and freshly ground pepper

1. If you are using a portobello, scoop out the dark brown gills with a teaspoon; they will darken the risotto. Trim the ends off the mushroom stem(s) and chop whichever you are using, the portobello or the white mushrooms.

2. Trim the tough ends off the asparagus. Thinly slice the stalks, including the tips, on an angle.

3. Heat the olive oil in your nonstick frying pan over medium-high heat. Add the onion and cook until soft and beginning to color, 3 to 4 minutes. Add the

mushrooms and cook until their liquid is released, about 4 minutes. Add the asparagus and sauté 2 minutes longer.

4. Add the rice and cook, stirring, for 1 minute. Pour in the wine and cook, stirring often, until it is absorbed. Pour in about 1 cup of the chicken broth. Reduce the heat to medium-low and cook, stirring often, until the broth is almost all absorbed. Continue gradually adding the broth and cooking until absorbed, until the rice is tender but still firm in the center and coated with a creamy sauce, about 20 minutes. If you run out of broth before the rice is done, add a little water.

5. Stir in the butter and then the cheese. Season with salt and pepper to taste. Serve the risotto at once.

SERVES 3 OR 4

Dr. Roland's Midnight Rice RX

My good friend Tom Roland is one of the top ear surgeons in the country. Because of the long hours he keeps, he often finds himself getting home late at night, tired and hungry and in no mood to eat cold chili out of a can. As a result, he has developed a repertoire of one-skillet rice dishes based largely on leftovers and ingredients commonly found in one's pantry.

Following are three of Tom's favorite quick and easy rice dishes. Each calls for two cups of cooked white rice. Because the idea here is to use ingredients already on hand, substitutes have been suggested for almost every key ingredient.

Curried Rice

2 tablespoons olive oil
I cup shredded cooked chicken, beef, or lamb
8 large white mushrooms, thinly sliced
I medium onion, chopped
2 teaspoons curry powder
2 cups cooked rice, preferably basmati
Mango chutney

1. Heat the olive oil in your nonstick frying pan over high heat. Add the shredded meat, mushrooms, and onion. Cook, tossing, until the meat is just crispy, about 5 minutes.

2. Add the curry powder and mix well. Stir in the rice. Cook, stirring often, until the rice turns slightly brown, about 5 minutes. Serve hot, with mango chutney.

SERVES 2

Mexican Black Beans and Rice

2 tablespoons olive oil

I cup shredded cooked chicken, pork, or beef (sliced sausages can also be
used)

I medium red bell pepper, thinly sliced, or for color use ½ red and ½ green
bell peppers

2 large tomatoes, diced, or I can (14½ ounces) stewed tomatoes

I cup canned black beans, rinsed and drained

2 cups cooked rice

I tablespoon chili powder

¼ cup fresh lime or lemon juice

I teaspoon hot pepper sauce, such as Tabasco, or I small jalapeño pepper,
seeded and minced

¼ teaspoon salt

⅛ teaspoon freshly ground pepper

¼ cup finely chopped cilantro or parsley

Salsa, guacamole, and/or sour cream (optional)

1. Heat the olive oil in your nonstick frying pan over high heat. Add the shredded meat, bell pepper, and tomatoes and cook, tossing constantly, until the pepper is softened and the tomatoes thicken slightly, about 4 minutes.

2. Add the black beans, rice, chili powder, lime juice, hot sauce, salt, and pepper. Cook, stirring, until the rice turns slightly brown, about 5 minutes.

3. Add the cilantro and cook, tossing, for 1 minute. Season with additional salt and pepper to taste. If you like, stir in salsa, guacamole or sour cream, or a combination of the three, or pass them on the side.

SERVES 2

CITRUS SHRIMP AND RICE

ONE-PAN
MEALS

148

¾ pound shrimp, peeled but with tails left on (size is up to you)
2 tablespoons olive oil
½ cup fresh lemon juice
2 teaspoons chili powder
I teaspoon honey, sugar, or maple syrup, or I tablespoon frozen lemonade
    concentrate
⅛ teaspoon freshly ground pepper
2 cups cooked rice

1. In a medium bowl, toss the shrimp with the olive oil. Heat your nonstick frying pan over high heat for 1 to 2 minutes. Add the shrimp and cook, tossing, for about 1 minute, until they are pink and loosely curled.

2. Add the lemon juice, chili powder, honey, and pepper. Stir to mix well. Add the rice and cook, stirring constantly, until it turns slightly brown, about 5 minutes. Serve at once.

SERVES 2

CINCINNATI CHILI

Somehow, as chili was passing through Ohio, a tributary broke off and headed straight for Cincinnati. This strange concoction is unlike any other chili you've ever tasted and is positively addictive. The "secret ingredient" is a chocolate bar!

Cincinnatians serve their chili over spaghetti topped with grated cheese and chopped onion, and accompany it with oyster or saltine crackers. The chili also works well over rice, doubles for sloppy joes, and makes a great taco filling.

I pound ground beef
I onion, chopped
2 celery ribs, chopped
2 garlic cloves, minced
I tablespoon chili powder
½ teaspoon ground cumin
½ teaspoon cinnamon
½ teaspoon salt
¼ teaspoon freshly ground pepper
I can (28 ounces) stewed tomatoes
½ cup beef broth
I tablespoon red wine vinegar
½ chocolate bar (2 ounces) like Hershey's (no almonds)

1. In your nonstick frying pan, cook the ground beef, onion, celery, and garlic over medium-high heat, stirring often to break up lumps of meat, until the beef loses its pink color, about 5 minutes. Add the chili powder, cumin, cinnamon, salt, and pepper. Cook, stirring, 1 minute.

2. Add the stewed tomatoes, beef broth, vinegar, and chocolate; cut up the tomatoes while cooking with a pair of kitchen scissors. Bring to a boil, reduce the heat to low, and simmer 1 hour, adding more beef broth if the chili gets too thick.

SERVES 4 TO 6

Five-Alarm Trail Drive Chili

Bacon drippings and strong java are the chuck-wagon touches that make this tasty, fiery chili special. Combining pork with beef also increases the depth of flavor. Some supermarkets stock ground pork, while at others you may need to order it in advance. In a pinch, mild Italian bulk sausage, preferably without fennel seeds, works well, too.

2 tablespoons bacon drippings or olive oil
2 cups chopped onions
4 garlic cloves, finely chopped
2 to 3 fresh jalapeño peppers, minced (include some or all of the ribs and
        seeds for maximum fire)
3 tablespoons medium-hot chili powder
¼ teaspoon ground cumin
¼ teaspoon dried oregano
I pound ground beef sirloin
I pound ground pork
I can (14½ ounces) beef broth
1¼ cups canned crushed tomatoes with added puree
¾ cup strong brewed coffee, preferably French roast
¾ teaspoon salt
½ teaspoon freshly ground black pepper
I can (15½ ounces) dark red kidney beans, rinsed and drained
2 tablespoons yellow cornmeal
Grated Cheddar or Jack cheese, chopped onions, pickled jalapeño slices,
        diced tomatoes, and sour cream, as accompaniments

1. In your nonstick frying pan, melt the bacon drippings over medium heat. Add the onions, garlic, jalapeños, chili powder, cumin, and oregano. Cover and cook, stirring occasionally, 8 to 10 minutes, or until the onions are golden.

2. Add the beef and pork. Raise the heat slightly and cook, uncovered, stirring and breaking up the lumps of meat, until it loses its raw color, about 10 minutes longer.

3. Add the broth, tomatoes, coffee, salt, and pepper to the pan. Bring to a simmer. Partially cover and cook, stirring occasionally, until the chili is thickened and flavorful, about 45 minutes.

4. Stir in the beans and cook for 3 minutes. Sprinkle the cornmeal over the chili. Stir it in and cook until the chili is thick, 2 to 3 minutes. Season with additional salt and pepper to taste. Serve hot, with accompaniments as desired.

SERVES 6

Vegetable Chili with Bulgur, Brown Rice, and Beans

Like many people my age, I find myself still loving a thick steak but turning away from meat completely at least several times a week. Since I love vegetables and pasta, the taste is easy; it's the texture that gives me pause. I still want a chewiness to my food, something of a meaty texture. That's where grains come in. Here I use two: bulgur, which is cracked wheat, readily available at supermarkets, and brown rice. The bulgur will soften in short order, but the brown rice takes about 40 minutes to cook, so that goes in first. This is really a one-dish meal. Serve it as is, or dress it up if you like with sour cream, shredded Cheddar cheese, and tortilla chips passed on the side.

2½ tablespoons olive oil

2 medium onions, chopped

2 celery ribs, chopped

4 garlic cloves, chopped

3 tablespoons chili powder

1 teaspoon ground cumin

½ teaspoon ground cinnamon

1 can (28 ounces) Italian peeled tomatoes, coarsely chopped, juices reserved

2 cups chicken or vegetable stock

2 cups chopped cabbage

2 carrots, peeled and chopped

1 green bell pepper, chopped

1 red bell pepper, chopped

⅓ cup brown rice

1 zucchini, chopped

1 yellow squash, chopped

⅓ cup bulgur

1 can (15 ounces) pinto beans or black beans, rinsed and drained

Salt and your favorite hot sauce

1. In your nonstick frying pan, heat the oil over medium-low heat. Add the onions and celery, cover, and cook 5 minutes to soften. Uncover, raise the heat to medium-high, and cook, stirring occasionally, until the onions are golden, 5 to 7 minutes.

2. Add the garlic, chili powder, cumin, and cinnamon. Cook, stirring, 1 minute. Pour in the tomatoes with their juices, the stock, and 1 cup water. Add the cabbage, carrots, and bell peppers. Bring to a boil. Stir in the brown rice, cover, reduce the heat to low, and cook for 30 minutes, or until the rice is about three-quarters cooked.

3. Add the zucchini, squash, and bulgur. Cover and cook 10 minutes. Stir in the beans and cook 5 minutes longer, or until the brown rice and bulgur are tender but still chewy. Season with salt and hot sauce to taste.

SERVES 6

Peppers Stuffed with Beef and Rice

To fit all four bell peppers in the pan, choose modestly sized ones and mound the filling up if you have to. I always serve Italian bread with this easy dish, to mop up any extra sauce. My only tip: Keep an eye on the pan during the last fifteen minutes or so of cooking and pour in an extra ¼ cup water if the sauce gets too thick.

4 medium-small green bell peppers
I tablespoon extra-virgin olive oil
I medium onion, chopped
I large garlic clove, minced
I pound lean ground beef
½ cup long-grain white rice
I teaspoon dried oregano
I teaspoon salt
¼ teaspoon freshly ground pepper
⅛ teaspoon Tabasco or other hot sauce, or more to taste
1½ cups prepared marinara or spaghetti sauce

1. Halve the bell peppers lengthwise. Remove the stems, seeds, and whitish inner ribs.

2. Heat the olive oil in your nonstick frying pan over medium heat. Add the onion and garlic. Cook, stirring, until golden, about 5 minutes. Scrape into a medium bowl and let cool slightly.

3. Add the ground beef and rice to the onion and garlic. Sprinkle on half the oregano, the salt, pepper, and Tabasco. Mix well with your hands to blend evenly. Lightly pack about ¼ cup of the stuffing into each pepper half.

4. Arrange the peppers in the same pan. Mix the marinara sauce with the remaining ½ teaspoon oregano and 1 cup water. Pour over and around the stuffed peppers. Bring the liquid to a simmer. Cover and reduce the heat to medium-low. Cook, basting the peppers occasionally with the sauce, until the peppers are tender but still hold their shape and the beef and rice are cooked through, 40 to 45 minutes.

SERVES 3 OR 4

Skillet Stuffed Cabbage

While getting this together takes a little extra work, it is one of those recipes that improves greatly when made several hours or a couple of days ahead. I like the extra boost of flavor a touch of sausage adds, but if you prefer, you can make the filling with all beef. Savory stuffed cabbage, with its slightly sweet-sour tomato sauce, makes great cold weather eating and needs only thick slabs of peasant or whole-grain bread to create a complete meal.

3 tablespoons olive oil
I medium onion, thinly sliced, plus ½ cup finely chopped onion
¾ pound ground beef round
¼ pound bulk pork sausage
½ cup long-grain white rice
I tablespoon chopped parsley
I¼ teaspoons salt
½ teaspoon freshly ground pepper
I (3-pound) cabbage
2 cans (14½ ounces each) diced tomatoes in juice
2 tablespoons cider vinegar
I½ tablespoons dark brown sugar
I bay leaf

1. In your nonstick frying pan, heat 1½ tablespoons of the olive oil. Add the chopped onion and cook over medium-high heat, stirring occasionally, until lightly browned, 3 to 4 minutes. Scrape into a medium bowl. Add the ground beef, sausage, raw rice, parsley, ¾ teaspoon of the salt, and ¼ teaspoon of the pepper. Using your hands, mix until evenly blended. Set the filling aside.

2. Bring a large saucepan of salted water to a boil over high heat. Remove and discard any tough, dark green outer leaves of the cabbage. Then carefully remove the 10 largest top leaves. Add the cabbage leaves 5 at a time to the

saucepan and boil until wilted, 2 to 3 minutes. Remove with tongs to a colander. Core the remaining cabbage and thinly slice into shreds.

3. Cut out a thin triangle from the thickest part of the rib at the base of each wilted cabbage leaf. Scoop 3 to 4 tablespoons of the filling onto each leaf. Fold in the sides and roll up to enclose the meat.

4. In your nonstick frying pan, heat the remaining 1½ tablespoons oil over medium-high heat. Add the sliced onion and cook for 1 to 2 minutes. Add half the shredded cabbage and sauté, stirring occasionally, until the cabbage is wilted and the onion is golden, about 3 minutes. Stir in the remaining shredded cabbage, salt, and pepper and continue to cook until all the cabbage is wilted, some of it is lightly colored, and the onion is golden brown, about 5 minutes longer.

5. Pour in the tomatoes with their juices. Stir in the vinegar and brown sugar and add the bay leaf. Arrange the stuffed cabbage rolls in the pan in a single layer. Spoon up some of the sautéed cabbage and onion over the rolls. Cover, reduce the heat to medium-low, and simmer 45 minutes, spooning some of the juice up over the rolls every 10 minutes or so.

6. Pour ¼ cup water into the pan. Let stand, covered, 15 minutes. Remove the bay leaf before serving.

SERVES 3 OR 4

Meatball and Carrot Ragout

Here is a pan full of sheer comfort. Not a pasta sauce, this is indeed a ragout, or stew, studded with tender meatballs and sweet carrots in a luscious, tomatoey gravy. The pan excels at this sort of browning-and-then-simmering process. For convenience, the entire dish can be prepared in advance, then carefully re-warmed for serving. Rice or pasta makes a more than acceptable starchy partner, but the ragout is really at its best spooned over a fluffy mound of your finest mashed potatoes.

3 tablespoons olive oil
1½ cups finely chopped onions
8 garlic cloves, finely chopped
1½ teaspoons dried basil
1 teaspoon dried oregano
½ teaspoon dried thyme leaves
½ teaspoon crushed hot red pepper
¾ pound ground beef, preferably chuck
¾ pound ground pork
⅓ cup fine dry bread crumbs
2 eggs, beaten
1 teaspoon salt
3 medium carrots (about ½ pound total), peeled and diced
2 tablespoons flour
1½ cups prepared tomato sauce, such as marinara
1 cup reduced-sodium canned chicken broth
½ cup dry red wine
⅓ cup finely chopped flat-leaf parsley

1. In your nonstick pan, warm 2 tablespoons of the oil over medium heat. Add the onions, garlic, basil, oregano, thyme, and hot pepper. Cover and cook, stir-

ring occasionally, for 8 to 10 minutes, or until the onions are golden. Remove from the heat and let cool to room temperature.

2. In a large bowl, combine the beef, pork, bread crumbs, eggs, half the onion mixture from the pan, and the salt. Mix thoroughly. Form the meat mixture into 24 balls, 1½ inches in diameter. Transfer them to a sheet pan as you go. Scrape the remaining onion mixture into a bowl; no need to clean the pan.

3. Set the pan over medium heat. Add about half the meatballs and cook, turning them occasionally and rearranging them to promote even cooking, until they are nicely browned, about 10 minutes (the meatballs will not be cooked through). Transfer to paper towels to drain. Repeat with the remaining meatballs. Pour off any drippings but do not clean the pan.

4. Add the remaining 1 tablespoon oil and the carrots. Cover and cook over medium heat, stirring occasionally, until the carrots are lightly colored and almost tender, about 15 minutes. Stir in the reserved onion mixture and cook 2 minutes. Sprinkle the flour over the vegetables and cook, stirring often, for 2 minutes. Stir in the tomato sauce, broth, and wine.

5. Add the browned meatballs to the sauce in the pan and bring to a simmer. Partially cover and cook, stirring occasionally, until the meatballs are cooked through and the gravy has thickened, about 15 minutes. Stir in the parsley and serve.

SERVES 6

WHITE PAN PIZZA

Given the popularity of grilled pizza, I decided to try and make pizza in the pan. Guess what—it works! What's especially nice about pan pizzas are the crisp olive oil–kissed edges around the dough and the fact that in warmer weather you can make this dish without preheating the oven. Gooey with cheese and fragrant from garlic and herbs, this simple pizza makes a fine supper when paired with a crisp green salad.

¼ cup olive oil
2 garlic cloves, crushed through a press
¼ teaspoon crushed hot red pepper
I pound frozen bread dough, thawed in the refrigerator
8 ounces shredded pizza cheese blend (about 2 cups)*
¾ teaspoon dried oregano

1. In a small bowl, combine 2 tablespoons of the olive oil, the garlic, and the hot pepper. Cover and let stand at room temperature for at least 30 minutes.

2. On a lightly floured work surface, pat and roll the dough out into a 12-inch round. Brush the inside of the pan with half the remaining olive oil. Transfer the dough to the pan. Let the dough rest for 30 minutes, patting it more evenly into the pan as it relaxes from handling.

3. Set the pan over low heat and cover. Rearrange the position of the pan on the burner to promote even cooking until the bottom of the dough is lightly but evenly browned, 12 to 15 minutes (lift it with a spatula to check from time to time).

4. Brush the top of the dough with the remaining oil. With a wide spatula, flip the dough over. Brush the browned top with the garlic-oil mixture. Scatter the cheese over the dough. Season with the oregano. Cover the pan and continue to

cook, rearranging its position on the burner, until the bottom is golden, the dough is cooked through, and the cheese has melted, another 10 minutes or so. Transfer to a carving board. Cut into wedges and serve while hot.

* A common supermarket brand of pizza cheese contains shredded mozzarella, provolone, Romano, and Parmesan. Or make your own mixture of about one-half mozzarella, one-quarter provolone, and one-eighth each Parmesan and Romano.

SERVES 2 AS A LIGHT MAIN COURSE

DOUBLE-CRUSTED TURKEY SAUSAGE PAN PIZZAS

In Italy, these stuffed, double-crusted fried pizzas are known as calzone or pan-zarotti. They're terrific both hot from the skillet and at room temperature. You can put them on a plate and eat them with a knife and fork. But the kids and I love to wrap them in paper towels and eat them out of hand. Needless to say, they make a really easy portable meal-to-go for picnics or long car trips. If you make the filling ahead of time—whether a few hours or a couple of days—the pizzas can be assembled and cooked in a flash in the pan.

1 tablespoon extra-virgin olive oil

½ pound Italian turkey sausage (hot or mild to your taste), casings removed

1 small onion, chopped

1 small green bell pepper, chopped

½ cup tomato puree

¼ cup chopped Italian parsley

4 ounces shredded mozzarella cheese (about 1 cup)

¼ cup freshly grated Parmesan cheese

1 pound prepared refrigerated or frozen pizza dough or homemade, risen once

1 cup canola oil

1. Heat the olive oil in your nonstick frying pan over medium-high heat. Crumble the turkey sausage into the pan and cook, stirring and breaking up the meat into small pieces with a wooden spoon, until no pink color remains, 4 to 5 minutes. Add the onion and bell pepper. Cook, stirring a few times, until the onion begins to turn golden.

2. Add the tomato puree to the pan. Bring to a boil, stirring to incorporate any brown bits from the bottom of the pan. Transfer to a bowl. Let cook, then stir in the parsley, mozzarella cheese, and Parmesan cheese. (The filling can be made

several hours ahead and set aside at room temperature or up to 2 days ahead and refrigerated. Let return to room temperature before using.)

3. On a lightly floured board, roll out the pizza dough to a 14-inch square about ¼ inch thick. Cut into 4 equal pieces to make four (7-inch) squares. Place one-fourth of the filling on half of each dough square. Fold the other half over the filling to make a rectangle. Press and crimp the edges together tightly with your fingers to seal.

4. Heat the canola oil in your nonstick frying pan over medium heat until it registers 350 degrees F on a frying thermometer. Gently slide 2 pizzas into the oil and fry, turning once, until golden brown, 2 to 3 minutes per side. Remove with a slotted spoon or spatula and drain on paper towels. Repeat with the remaining 2 pizzas.

SERVES 4

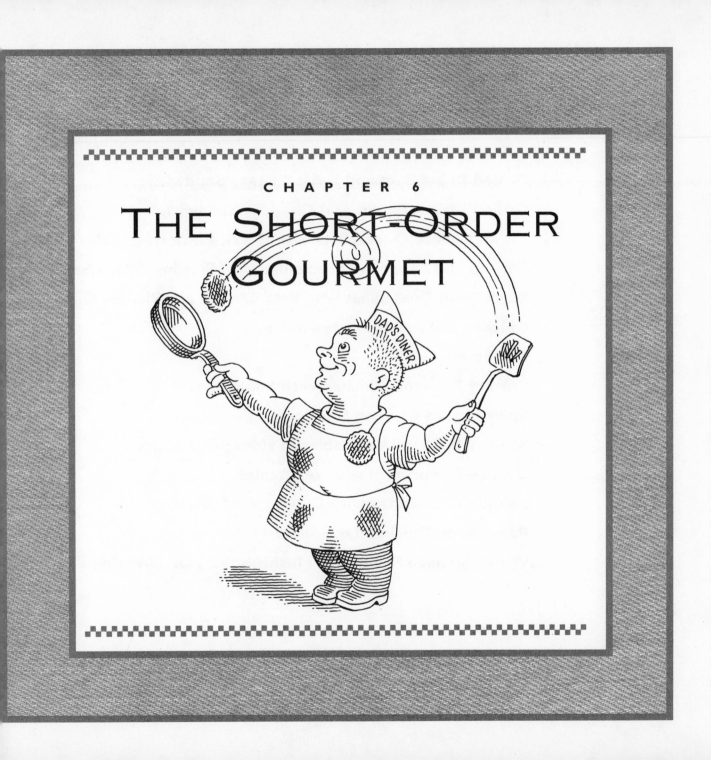

CHAPTER 6

THE SHORT-ORDER GOURMET

California Turkey Burgers

Beef Burgers with Browned Onions and Brandy-Roquefort Butter

Grilled Roast Beef and Swiss Cheese Sandwiches

Grilled Turkey, Bacon, and Cheddar Sandwiches

Three-Cheese Quesadillas with Quick Black Bean Salsa

Shrimp and Avocado Quesadillas with Sizzling Green Salsa

Black Bean Quesadillas with Feta Cheese and Pico de Gallo

Chicken and Artichoke Hash

Red Flannel Hash

Stir-Fry Jalapeño Chicken with Snow Peas

Spicy Peanut Chicken Stir-Fry

Stir-Fry Beef and Vegetables in Honey-Tea Sauce

Orange-Flavor Pork with Vegetables

Salmon Croquettes with Dill-Mustard Sauce

Pan-Seared Chicken Taco Salad

Warm Spinach Salad with Mushroom-Bacon Dressing

CALIFORNIA TURKEY BURGERS

California, the land of light, healthful eating, is also the land of the creatively overstuffed burger. How to blend the two? One way is a panful of these moist, well-browned turkey burgers. Stacked onto buns with plenty of tasty, crunchy additions, they take two hands to handle.

¾ pound ground turkey
2 teaspoons olive oil
Salt and freshly ground pepper
3 ounces thinly sliced jalapeño Jack cheese
2 large, premium whole-grain hamburger buns or sandwich rolls
4 teaspoons mayonnaise
4 thin slices of ripe avocado
2 thin slices from a large tomato
About 1½ ounces sunflower (aka stir-fry) sprouts

1. Divide the ground turkey in half and form each half into a ¾-inch-thick patty about 5 inches in diameter. Cover and refrigerate if not cooking immediately.

2. In your nonstick frying pan, warm the oil over medium heat. When it is hot, add the patties. Cook until well browned on the bottom, about 6 minutes. Turn over, season to taste with salt and pepper, and continue to cook until cooked through but still juicy in the center, 6 to 8 minutes; do not serve undercooked turkey. About 4 minutes before you estimate the burgers will be done, top them with the cheese and cover the pan.

3. Meanwhile, toast the buns if desired. Spread the bun bottoms with the mayonnaise. When the turkey is cooked through, set the burgers on the bun bottoms. Top with the avocado, tomato slices, and sprouts. Set the bun tops in place and serve immediately.

MAKES 2 SANDWICHES

BEEF BURGERS WITH BROWNED ONIONS AND BRANDY-ROQUEFORT BUTTER

Beef and blue cheese is an honorable combo, no matter how you assemble the team. This pan-pairing is weeknight casual, but the kind of no-ketchup, no-pickles deal that kids won't like at all. Order them a pizza and make the burgers for the grown-ups. Since the flavor profile is vaguely French, I like to serve French fries and a green salad and pour a good red wine.

½ **pound good-quality Roquefort or other blue cheese, at room temperature**
2 **tablespoons unsalted butter, softened**
3 **tablespoons brandy**
½ **teaspoon hot pepper sauce, such as Tabasco**
2 **teaspoons vegetable oil**
4 **(½-inch-thick) slices from a very large onion**
4 **teaspoons balsamic vinegar**
1½ **pounds ground beef, preferably chuck, formed into 4¾-inch-thick patties**
    about 5 inches in diameter
Salt and freshly ground black pepper
4 **large premium hamburger buns, about 5 inches in diameter, split and**
    lightly toasted
4 **(¼-inch-thick) slices from a very large ripe tomato**
½ **bunch watercress, coarse stems trimmed**

1. In a medium bowl, mash together the cheese and butter. Add the brandy and pepper sauce and stir until fairly smooth. Cover and refrigerate the Roquefort butter until using.

2. In your nonstick frying pan, warm the oil over medium heat. Add the onion slices and cook until browned on the bottom, 4 to 5 minutes. Drizzle each slice with 1 teaspoon of the vinegar, turn over, and cook until lightly browned, another 5 minutes or so. Transfer to a plate. Do not clean the pan.

3. Set the pan over medium heat. When it is hot, add the beef patties. Cook until browned on the bottom, about 4 minutes. Turn, season lightly with salt and pepper, top with the browned onion slices, and continue to cook until the patties are well browned on the second side and done to your liking, about 4 minutes for medium-rare.

4. Meanwhile, spread the bun tops with the Roquefort butter. Set the burger on each bun bottom. Top each burger with a slice of tomato and sprigs of watercress. Set the bun tops in place and serve immediately.

SERVES 4

GRILLED ROAST BEEF AND SWISS CHEESE SANDWICHES

Designed to go with beer, these big, gutsy, pan-griddled sandwiches are perfect enjoyed in front of the television (with plenty of napkins). I like them best made with home-cooked pot roast, preferably brisket, but good-quality deli roast beef works great, too.

4 (6-inch) slices of good-quality rye or pumpernickel sandwich bread
¼ cup prepared horseradish sauce
6 ounces thinly sliced Swiss cheese
½ pound thinly sliced roast beef
Salt
10 dill pickle chips, patted dry
3 tablespoons unsalted butter, at room temperature

1. Lay the bread slices on a flat work surface. Spread some of the horseradish sauce over one side of each bread slice. Arrange half the cheese evenly over 2 slices of bread, trimming the cheese to fit. Top the cheese with the beef. Season lightly with salt. Arrange the pickle slices over the beef, dividing them evenly. Top with the remaining cheese, trimming it to fit if necessary. Set the remaining bread slices atop the cheese, sauce side down. Spread the tops of the sandwiches with half the butter, dividing it evenly.

2. Set your nonstick frying pan over medium-low heat. Set the sandwiches in the pan, buttered sides down. Brush the tops of the sandwiches with the remaining butter. Cover the pan and cook, turning once, until the sandwiches are crisp and well browned and the cheese has melted, 4 to 5 minutes on each side.

3. Transfer the grilled sandwiches to a cutting board. Cut in half and serve while hot.

MAKES 2 SANDWICHES

Grilled Turkey, Bacon, and Cheddar Sandwiches

Derived from the classic club sandwich, these are hearty and, thanks to the browning capabilities of the pan, satisfyingly crusty. Though mayo works on a club, here you want something sharp and sweet, to provide contrast to the smoky meats. The solution is honey mustard—choose a good, spicy one and don't be stingy.

2 slices of thick-cut bacon, halved crosswise
4 (6-inch) slices of good-quality sandwich bread, such as sourdough
⅓ cup honey mustard
6 ounces thinly sliced sharp Cheddar cheese
4 very thin slices of tomato
½ pound thinly sliced smoked turkey breast
3 tablespoons unsalted butter, softened

1. Cook the bacon in your nonstick frying pan over medium heat until lightly browned and crisp, 6 to 8 minutes. Drain the bacon on paper towels. Pour off the drippings and wipe out the pan.

2. Lay the bread slices on a work surface. Spread with the mustard. Arrange half the cheese evenly over 2 slices of bread. Lay the tomato slices over the cheese. Then add the turkey, ruffling the slices to fit. Top the turkey with the bacon. Cover the bacon with the remaining cheese. Set the remaining bread slices atop the cheese, mustard side down. Spread half the butter over the tops of the sandwiches.

3. Set the pan over medium-low heat. Set the sandwiches in the pan, buttered sides down. Spread the remaining butter over the tops of the sandwiches. Cover the pan and cook, turning once, until the sandwiches are crisp and well browned and the cheese is melted, 4 to 5 minutes per side. Transfer the grilled sandwiches to a cutting board. Let stand for about 1 minute, then cut in half and serve.

MAKES 2 SANDWICHES

THREE-CHEESE QUESADILLAS WITH QUICK BLACK BEAN SALSA

Here the pan functions like the Mexican griddle known as a *comal*. With only a hint of nonstick spray, gooey cheese-filled flour tortilla "sandwiches" cook up crisp and brown in only minutes. Dolloped with an almost-instant bean salsa, they're great as snacks, swell alongside scrambled eggs, and unbeatable as a kind of Tex-Mex grilled cheese sandwich. These three cheeses work for me, but clean out the fridge and use what you will.

I jar (16 ounces) salsa (choose your favorite level of heat)
I can (15 ounces) black beans, rinsed and drained
⅓ cup chopped red onion
⅓ cup finely chopped cilantro
6 ounces mild white goat cheese, at room temperature
8 large flour tortillas, 10 inches in diameter
1⅓ cups shredded sharp Cheddar cheese (about 5½ ounces)
1⅓ cups shredded jalapeño Jack cheese (about 5½ ounces)

1. In a bowl, stir together the salsa, black beans, red onion, and cilantro. Cover and refrigerate the salsa if not using immediately.

2. Spread one-fourth of the goat cheese evenly over 1 tortilla. Scatter one-fourth of the Cheddar and one-fourth of the Jack cheese over the goat cheese. Top with a second tortilla. Repeat with the remaining tortillas and cheese, assembling 4 quesadillas in all.

3. Lightly coat your nonstick frying pan with nonstick spray and set over medium heat. With a large spatula, transfer 1 quesadilla to the hot skillet. Weight with a small flat heatproof plate and cover the pan. Cook until the bottom is lightly browned, 2 to 3 minutes. Remove the plate, flip the quesadilla

over, weight again with the plate, cover, and continue to cook until the cheeses are melted and bubbling and the bottom tortilla is lightly browned, another 2 to 3 minutes.

4. Keep the finished quesadillas warm in the oven until all are done, or serve as you go. To serve, transfer the quesadillas to a board, cut into wedges (use a long knife or a pizza wheel), and enjoy hot. Pass the black bean salsa on the side.

SERVES 4 AS A MAIN COURSE, 6 TO 8 AS AN APPETIZER OR ACCOMPANIMENT

Shrimp and Avocado Quesadillas with Sizzling Green Salsa

A great quick snack or light lunch. As an appetizer, quesadillas can be cut into wedges to serve six. Since the pan has a nonstick surface, a vegetable oil–based cooking spray is all you need to soften the tortillas in the pan. If you're counting fat calories, use a light sour cream or omit it entirely.

½ pound cooked peeled shrimp
2 tablespoons finely chopped white onion
2 tablespoons chopped cilantro (if you have it)
1 lime
Salt and freshly ground pepper
6 corn tortillas
1 ripe avocado, sliced
1 cup shredded Cheddar or mozzarella cheese
Sizzling Green Salsa (recipe follows) or your favorite bottled salsa and
    sour cream

1. Slice the shrimp lengthwise in half and then cut them crosswise into 2 or 3 pieces. Place in a bowl and toss with the onion, cilantro, and the juice of half the lime. Season with salt and pepper to taste.

2. Coat your nonstick frying pan lightly with cooking spray and heat over medium-high heat. Add 1 tortilla. Cook 30 seconds, then flip over. Quickly layer one-third of shrimp and one-third of the avocado slices on the tortilla, leaving a ½-inch margin around the edges. Sprinkle ⅓ cup of the shredded cheese on top. Cover with another tortilla and press lightly.

3. Cook until the bottom of the tortilla is lightly browned, 1 to 2 minutes. Turn carefully with a wide spatula and cook until the second side is lightly colored and the cheese is melted, 1 to 2 minutes longer. Slide the quesadilla onto a plate.

4. Repeat to make 2 more quesadillas. Cut them into quarters or into 6 wedges each. Serve with wedges cut from the remaining lime half and dollops of salsa and sour cream.

SERVES 3

SIZZLING GREEN SALSA

Technically, *salsa* is just the Spanish word for sauce, but you just know there's more kick to it than that. This one is made from fresh tomatillos—those hard Mexican green tomato-like things that come with their own papery wrapper—and chiles. While the sauce is okay *crudo,* or raw, it's much better and more mellow when flash-fried in your pan for just a few minutes. The nonstick surface makes it easy to do without adding a lot of fat. Use this terrific, all-purpose salsa for dipping tortilla chips or shrimp or as a sauce with chicken or cheese enchiladas.

1 pound fresh tomatillos
½ medium white onion, cut up
2 garlic cloves, coarsely chopped
2 jalapeño or serrano chiles*
1½ tablespoons corn, peanut, or olive oil
¾ cup chicken broth, homemade or reduced-sodium canned
⅓ cup heavy cream
Salt
⅓ cup chopped cilantro

1. Peel the papery outer husks off the tomatillos. Rinse the tomatillos and pat dry. Cut into quarters and place in a food processor. Add the onion and garlic. Remove the stems and slice the chiles. Add them to the processor. Pulse, turning the machine quickly on and off, until the ingredients are finely chopped.

2. Heat the oil in your nonstick frying pan over high heat. Scrape the salsa into the skillet; it may splatter, so be careful. Cook, stirring with a wooden spoon or turning with a plastic spatula, until the mixture lightens in color slightly, about 2 minutes.

3. Add the chicken broth and boil, stirring until the salsa thickens slightly, about 3 minutes. Add the cream and boil 1 to 2 minutes longer.

4. Remove from the heat. Season with salt to taste. Stir in the cilantro shortly before using.

* In general, jalapeño peppers are milder than serrano chiles. If you prefer your salsa less fiery, remove the seeds and inner fibrous ribs from the chiles before slicing them.

MAKES ABOUT 1½ CUPS

Black Bean Quesadillas with Feta Cheese and Pico de Gallo

1 medium onion, chopped

2 tablespoons olive oil

1 green bell pepper, chopped

1 or 2 fresh jalapeño peppers, seeded and minced

1½ teaspoons whole cumin seeds

1 can (15 ounces) black beans, rinsed and drained

1 tablespoon chopped pickled jalapeño peppers

1 tablespoon sherry wine vinegar or red wine vinegar

Salt and freshly ground pepper

8 corn tortillas

½ cup crumbled feta cheese

Pico de gallo or your favorite tomato salsa

1. In your nonstick frying pan, cook the onion in the oil over medium-high heat until it is softened and beginning to brown, about 5 minutes. Add the bell pepper, fresh jalapeño(s), and cumin seeds. Cook, stirring 2 to 3 minutes, until the peppers are bright green and the seeds are lightly browned and fragrant.

2. Add the black beans, reduce the heat to medium, and cook, mashing some of them with a spatula or fork for a couple of minutes to mix them with the ingredients already in the pan. Add ½ cup of water, the pickled jalapeños, and the vinegar and continue to cook, stirring and mashing, until the beans are fairly dry again, about 5 minutes. Remove from the heat and season with salt and pepper to taste. Scrape the black beans into a bowl and wipe out the pan.

3. Lay 4 of the tortillas flat in front of you. Divide the black beans among the tortillas, leaving a ½-inch margin around the edges. Sprinkle about 2 tablespoons cheese over each. Cover with the remaining 4 tortillas and press lightly around the edges. Don't worry if this seal isn't perfect.

4. Coat the pan lightly with oil, using a vegetable spray or a little additional olive oil. One at a time, cook the quesadillas over medium heat until lightly browned on the bottom, about 2 minutes. Turn over with a wide spatula, press lightly, and cook until the second side is lightly browned, 1 to 2 minutes longer. Serve while hot. Pass the pico de gallo or salsa on the side.

SERVES 4

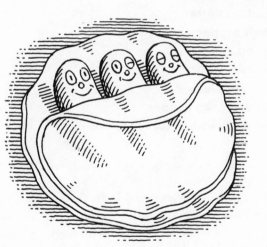

CHICKEN AND ARTICHOKE HASH

Hash made from scratch rather than with leftovers is a treat these days, particularly when it includes such a winning flavor combination. I like this dish so much and make it so often that tossing a chicken into the oven to roast first is no big deal (and the hash is moister made with fresh meat). But, if time is tight, don't hesitate to use a rotisserie bird from the supermarket or leftover chicken (or turkey) from the fridge. Only one rule: The artichokes must be fresh!

4 large artichokes
Salt
1 large red potato, peeled
4 tablespoons unsalted butter
¾ cup diced red bell pepper
½ cup chopped onion
2 garlic cloves, minced
¼ teaspoon dried thyme leaves
¼ teaspoon crushed hot red pepper
3 cups diced cooked chicken or turkey meat
1 tablespoon flour
½ cup heavy cream

1. Bring a very large pot of water to a boil. Add the artichokes and 1 tablespoon salt, partially cover, and cook until a knife easily pierces the stems, about 25 minutes. Drain and cool the artichokes. Trim about ½ inch off the stem ends, remove the leaves, scoop out the chokes, and cut the hearts into ½-inch pieces.

2. In a medium saucepan, cover the potato with cold water. Add 1 tablespoon salt, bring to a boil, and cook, partially covered, until just tender, about 40 minutes. Drain and let cool. Cut the potato into ½-inch dice.

3. In your nonstick frying pan, melt the butter over medium heat. Add the red bell pepper, onion, garlic, thyme, and hot pepper. Cover and cook, stirring once or twice, until the onion is lightly colored, 8 to 10 minutes. Add the chicken, artichokes, and potato. Sprinkle the flour and ¼ teaspoon salt over everything and cook, stirring often, for 2 minutes. Stir in the cream. Pat the chicken mixture into an even layer and cover the pan.

4. Set the pan slightly off center on the burner and cook, without stirring, until well browned, about 5 minutes (use a spatula to check). Continue to move the pan around on the burner until all parts have been directly over the center of the burner and the hash is evenly browned all over, another 15 to 20 minutes. To serve, lift the hash with a spatula and invert to a plate, its browned side up.

SERVES 4

Red Flannel Hash

In order to embrace this dish you will have to get used to the idea of a rather shocking pink batch of hash. Manage that, however, and you have some seriously delicious and rib-sticking fare ahead of you. This is suppertime hash at my house, designed to use up the leftovers from a big braised brisket or corned beef dinner.

3 tablespoons unsalted butter
1 medium onion, finely chopped
4 cups finely diced cooked beef brisket or corned beef (about 1 pound)
3 cooked red potatoes (about 1½ pounds total), peeled and finely diced
1 cooked medium beet, peeled and finely diced
¾ teaspoon salt
½ teaspoon freshly ground pepper
2 tablespoons flour
⅓ cup canned beef broth (or use leftover gravy from the brisket)
⅓ cup heavy cream

1. Melt the butter in your nonstick frying pan over medium heat. Add the onion, cover, and cook, stirring once or twice, until golden, 5 to 7 minutes. Add the brisket, potatoes, beet, salt, and pepper. Cover and cook, stirring occasionally, for 15 minutes.

2. Sprinkle the flour over the hash and stir it in. Cook, stirring once or twice, for 4 minutes. Stir in the broth and cream. Cover and cook the hash without stirring it, moving the pan around on the burner to promote even cooking and gently shaking it back and forth to prevent sticking, until it is crusty and well browned all over the bottom, 15 to 20 minutes. Serve hot, turning the crusty bottom upward as you spoon the hash from the pan.

SERVES 4 TO 6

Stir-Fry Jalapeño Chicken with Snow Peas

Here's a light, quick stir-fry, double heated with Chinese chili paste and jalapeño peppers.

1 pound boneless, skinless chicken breasts, cut into ½-inch slices
1 egg white
1 tablespoon cornstarch
⅓ cup chicken broth
1 tablespoon rice vinegar
1 tablespoon Chinese chili paste with garlic
2 tablespoons canola or corn oil
¼ pound snow peas, strings removed
2 scallions, sliced
2 jalapeño peppers, seeded and minced

1. Place the chicken in a heavy-duty plastic Ziploc bag or medium bowl. Add the egg white and cornstarch. Toss to coat. Seal the bag or cover the bowl with plastic wrap and marinate at room temperature for 15 to 30 minutes.

2. In a small bowl, mix the chicken broth, vinegar, and chili paste. Set the sauce aside.

3. Heat 1 tablespoon oil in your nonstick frying pan over high heat. Add the chicken and stir-fry until white throughout but still moist, 3 to 4 minutes. Remove to a bowl.

4. Add the remaining 1 tablespoon oil to the pan and heat over medium-high heat. Add the snow peas, scallions, and jalapeños. Stir-fry until the scallions begin to color, 2 to 3 minutes. Return the chicken to the pan. Stir in the reserved sauce and cook, tossing until the dish is very hot, 1 to 2 minutes.

SERVES 4

SPICY PEANUT CHICKEN STIR-FRY

This is my home skillet version of Kung Pao chicken, a spicy staple of Chinese delivery. Making it yourself from scratch means it's fresher, and, since you don't have to tip, cheaper as well. (Also, when you get good at all the chopping and dicing, it will be nearly as quick.) This is indeed picante; serve plenty of steamed white rice and drink beer or a chilled, not-too-dry white wine.

**2 large, whole skinless, boneless chicken breasts (about 1¾ pounds total), cut
    into ½-inch dice**
¼ cup dry sherry
2 tablespoons soy sauce
5 teaspoons Asian sesame oil
5 teaspoons finely chopped fresh ginger
3 garlic cloves, peeled and finely chopped
1 tablespoon plus 1 teaspoon cornstarch
**½ cup prepared Kung Pao sauce, available in many supermarkets and in
    Asian groceries**
¼ cup chicken broth
1 tablespoon packed dark brown sugar
4 scallions, cut on an angle into ½-inch pieces
¼ cup peanut oil
1 medium red bell pepper, cut into thin strips
**7 large fresh shiitake mushrooms (about 3 ounces), stems discarded, caps
    cut into sixths**
1 can (8 ounces) sliced water chestnuts, drained
1 cup lightly salted hulled peanuts, dry-roasted if desired

1. In a medium bowl, toss the chicken with 2 tablespoons of the sherry, the soy sauce, 1 tablespoon of the sesame oil, 2 teaspoons of the ginger, one-third of the garlic, and 1 tablespoon of the cornstarch. Toss well.

2. In a small bowl, mix the Kung Pao sauce into the remaining 1 teaspoon cornstarch. Whisk in the chicken broth, brown sugar, and the remaining 2 tablespoons sherry and 2 teaspoons sesame oil.

3. In another small bowl, combine the scallions, remaining 1 tablespoon ginger, and remaining garlic.

4. Set your nonstick frying pan over medium-high heat. When it is hot, add 2 tablespoons of the oil. Tilt the pan to coat it evenly. Add the chicken mixture and cook, tossing and stirring often, until the chicken cubes are firm, separate, and no longer pink outside (they will still be slightly underdone inside), about 3 minutes. Transfer the contents of the skillet to a strainer set over a bowl and let the excess oil drip off.

5. Reduce the heat to medium. Add the remaining 2 tablespoons peanut oil and the pepper strips to the pan. Cook, tossing and stirring often, for 1 minute. Add the mushrooms and the scallion mixture and cook, tossing and stirring, until the mushrooms are almost tender, about 2 minutes. Add the water chestnuts and the sauce mixture and bring to a simmer. Stir in the chicken and peanuts and continue to toss and stir often, until the sauce has thickened and the chicken is just cooked through while remaining moist, about 2 minutes.

SERVES 4

STIR-FRY BEEF AND VEGETABLES IN HONEY-TEA SAUCE

There's something almost magical about whipping up your own Chinese food at home. With the pan, even if you don't have a wok, you can stir-fry with aplomb. I like to get everything chopped up and measured out in advance. I make a big pot of rice to serve alongside. Then at the last minute, often with the family looking on, I pull out the pan and go to it. The final stir-fry takes only five minutes. Any kind of regular tea will do here. If you brew a pot at breakfast or in the late afternoon, save a cup to use in this aromatic marinade.

1 cup cold brewed tea
2 tablespoons honey
2 tablespoons soy sauce
1 tablespoon minced fresh ginger
2 garlic cloves, crushed through a press
1 pound flank steak, cut crosswise on an angle into thin slices
2 tablespoons peanut or other vegetable oil
2 carrots, sliced on an angle
2 onions, cut into large dice
2 tablespoons Chinese fermented black beans—rinsed, drained, and coarsely chopped
¼ teaspoon crushed hot red pepper
½ cup cooked broccoli florets (optional but nice for color)
1 teaspoon cornstarch

1. In a medium bowl, whisk together the tea, honey, soy sauce, half the ginger, and half the garlic. Add the flank steak and stir to coat. Cover and marinate at room temperature for 30 to 60 minutes or in the refrigerator for several hours.

2. Remove the meat from the marinade and drain on paper towels. Strain the marinade and reserve ¾ cup.

3. Set your nonstick frying pan over high heat until hot. Add 1 tablespoon of the oil. As soon as it is hot, add the carrots and onions. Cook, stirring and tossing, until the vegetables are crisp-tender and the onions are lightly colored around the edges, 3 to 4 minutes. Transfer to a bowl.

4. Heat the remaining 1 tablespoon oil in the same pan. Add the remaining ginger and garlic, the black beans, and the hot pepper. Stir-fry for 20 to 30 minutes, until fragrant. Add the beef and cook, tossing, until the meat is lightly browned, 3 to 4 minutes.

5. Return the carrots and onions to the pan. Add the broccoli. Stir the cornstarch into the reserved marinade. Pour into the pan and bring to a boil, stirring and tossing, until the sauce is thickened and everything is hot, about 1 minute. Serve at once.

SERVES 4 TO 6

ORANGE-FLAVOR PORK WITH VEGETABLES

All it takes to have fresh, high-quality Chinese food at home is the patience to do a little advance prep work. A few supermarket ingredients supply the necessary authentic flavor, and the pan more than capably stands in for the traditional wok. Serve this with lots of steamed white rice.

**2 small pork tenderloins (about ¾ pound each), trimmed and cut into ½-inch
  chunks**
⅓ cup dry sherry
¼ cup soy sauce
1 tablespoon Asian dark sesame oil
2 tablespoons minced fresh ginger
1 tablespoon plus 1½ teaspoons cornstarch
¾ cup reduced-sodium canned chicken broth
2 tablespoons fresh orange juice
5 garlic cloves, crushed through a press
1 tablespoon plus 1 teaspoon light brown sugar
1 tablespoon rice vinegar
1 tablespoon minced orange zest
¼ teaspoon freshly ground black pepper
3 tablespoons peanut oil
½ to ¾ teaspoon crushed hot red pepper, to taste
2 cups cooked frozen Asian vegetable medley

1. In a medium bowl, combine the chunks of pork, 2 tablespoons of the sherry, 2 tablespoons of the soy sauce, 1½ teaspoons of the sesame oil, the ginger, and 1 tablespoon of the cornstarch. Cover and let stand at room temperature, stirring once or twice, for 30 minutes.

2. In a small bowl, combine the remaining sherry, soy sauce, and cornstarch with the remaining sesame oil, the chicken broth, orange juice, garlic, brown sugar, vinegar, orange zest, and black pepper.

3. Set your nonstick frying pan over high heat. When it is very hot, add 2 tablespoons of the peanut oil. When the oil is very hot, add the pork. Cook, tossing and stirring often, until lightly browned and almost cooked through, about 5 minutes. With a slotted spoon, transfer the pork to a strainer set over a bowl to drain of any excess fat. Rinse and dry the pan.

4. Return the pan to high heat. When it is very hot, add the remaining 1 tablespoon oil. Add the hot pepper and cook, stirring, for 30 seconds. Add the vegetable medley and cook, tossing and stirring, for 30 seconds. Add the chicken broth mixture and bring to a simmer, stirring often. Add the pork and simmer, stirring occasionally, until the sauce has thickened, the pork is cooked through with no trace of pink in the center, and all ingredients are hot, 3 to 4 minutes longer.

SERVES 4

Salmon Croquettes with Dill-Mustard Sauce

I make this the day after we've had salmon for dinner, whether poached, sautéed, or grilled, and I recommend using leftover fresh whenever possible. However, in a pinch canned can, as they say, substitute. In fact, it will make these taste more like the croquettes of your childhood. For a really old-fashioned down-home meal, serve with creamed peas, rice pilaf, and piping hot biscuits.

2 cups flaked cooked fresh or canned salmon
⅓ cup sour cream
⅓ cup mayonnaise
I tablespoon mustard
¾ teaspoon hot pepper sauce, such as Tabasco
I tablespoon chopped fresh dill, plus sprigs of dill for garnish
2 eggs
½ cup lightly packed fresh bread crumbs
¼ cup minced onion
¼ cup minced celery
¼ teaspoon salt
I tablespoon unsalted butter
I tablespoon vegetable oil

1. Pick over the salmon to be sure there are no bits of skin or bone. In a small bowl, whisk together the sour cream, mayonnaise, mustard, and ¼ teaspoon hot sauce until well blended. Measure 2 tablespoons of this mixture into a larger bowl. Stir the chopped dill into the remaining sauce and set aside.

2. Beat the eggs into the 2 tablespoons sauce. Add the bread crumbs, onion, celery, salt, and remaining ½ teaspoon hot sauce. Mix well. Add the flaked

salmon and stir until evenly combined. Form the salmon mixture into 8 equal balls, transferring them to a plate as you go.

3. In your nonstick frying pan, melt the butter in the oil over medium heat. Add the salmon balls. Press them with a wide spatula to flatten slightly. Cook until well browned on the bottom. Turn over and continue to cook until browned on the second side and cooked through, 4 to 5 minutes longer.

4. Transfer the croquettes to plates and garnish with sprigs of dill. Pass the dill-mustard sauce on the side.

SERVES 4

PAN-SEARED CHICKEN TACO SALAD

Here's a cross between a skillet supper and a salad—with all the big Southwestern flavors that make food so pleasurable to eat. The ingredient list looks long, but everything is thrown together quickly and easily. Serve the salad with a basket of tortilla chips, a dish of sour cream, and an assortment of hot sauces. And for me—ice cold beer, please.

1 pound skinless, boneless chicken breasts
1 teaspoon ground cumin
½ teaspoon hot paprika
½ teaspoon dried oregano
½ teaspoon coarse salt
3 tablespoons extra-virgin olive oil
1 lime, quartered
½ head of iceberg lettuce, coarsely shredded
2 medium tomatoes, cut into ½-inch dice
1 can (15 ounces) pinto beans, rinsed and drained
1 can (11 ounces) corn niblets, drained
½ cup shredded Cheddar or Monterey Jack cheese
2 tablespoons sliced pickled jalapeño peppers, coarsely chopped
1 tablespoon rice vinegar
½ medium white onion, cut into ½-inch dice
½ large green bell pepper, cut into ½-inch dice
½ large red bell pepper, cut into ½-inch dice
2 garlic cloves, finely chopped

1. Trim off any fat or gristle from the chicken. If the chicken breasts have the tenders attached, remove the little white tendons and open them out so the meat is flatter and more even. Season on both sides with the cumin, hot paprika, oregano, and salt. Drizzle 2 teaspoons of olive oil and the juice from ¼ lime over

the chicken. Set aside at room temperature to marinate for up to 30 minutes while you prepare the rest of the salad.

2. In a large salad bowl, combine the lettuce, tomatoes, beans, corn, cheese, and pickled jalapeños. Add the rice vinegar and 1 tablespoon olive oil and toss to mix.

3. In your nonstick frying pan, heat the remaining oil over medium-high heat. Add the chicken breasts and sauté, turning once, until lightly browned outside and just cooked through and white inside but still juicy, 3 to 5 minutes per side. With tongs, remove the chicken to a cutting board and let rest.

4. Add the onion to the skillet and sauté for 1 minute. Add the green and red bell peppers and the garlic and cook, stirring, 1 to 2 minutes longer, until the peppers are brightly colored but still crisp. Remove from the heat.

5. Cut the chicken into bite-size chunks. Return to the skillet and toss with the onion and peppers. Scrape over the salad. Add an additional sprinkling of salt and the remaining lime juice. Toss and serve.

SERVES 4

Warm Spinach Salad with Mushroom-Bacon Dressing

The scent of the tart, warm dressing on this classic salad is a real appetite rouser. It's an easy salad, with a natural do-ahead break built in, but there is one tip I share to insure your success: To make the salad outstanding, buy the best, smokiest bacon you can.

6 slices of thick-cut bacon, cut crosswise into ½-inch strips
I bag (10 ounces) fresh spinach, preferably prewashed baby spinach leaves
3 tablespoons corn oil
I small onion, chopped
6 ounces medium-size brown (cremini) or white mushrooms, trimmed and
　　quartered
Salt
½ cup red wine vinegar
I tablespoon sugar
Freshly ground pepper

1. Place the bacon in your nonstick frying pan and set over medium heat. Cook, stirring occasionally, until the pieces have rendered most of their fat but are not brittle, 5 to 7 minutes. With a slotted spoon, transfer the bacon to paper towels to drain. Pour off all but 1 tablespoon of the drippings from the pan. (The recipe can be prepared to this point several hours in advance. Do not refrigerate the bacon.)

2. If the spinach is not trimmed and washed, remove the tough stems. Rinse well and spin dry. Place the spinach in a very large bowl.

3. Set the pan over medium heat and add the corn oil. When the pan is hot, add the onion. Cover and cook, stirring once or twice and scraping the bottom of the pan, until the onion is softened and translucent, about 5 minutes. Add the

mushrooms and ¼ teaspoon salt, cover, and cook, stirring once or twice, until the mushrooms begin to give up their juices, about 5 minutes. Uncover the pan, raise the heat to high, and sauté, stirring often, until most of the mushroom liquid has evaporated, about 1 minute.

4. In a small bowl, combine the vinegar and sugar. Add to the pan and bring to a boil, stirring often. Immediately pour the hot dressing over the spinach. Toss well. Season lightly with salt and generously with pepper and toss again. Add the bacon and toss a final time. Serve immediately.

SERVES 4

CHAPTER 7

SIDES FOR ALL OCCASIONS

Southwestern Red Beans and Rice

Hash Brown Potatoes with Onions and Peppers

Roquefort Potato Cakes with Browned Onions

Potato, Carrot, and Celery Root Pancakes

Buttermilk-Scallion Hush Puppies

Cheesy Polenta in the Pan

Sautéed Artichoke Hearts with Melted Fontina Cheese

Stir-Fried Asparagus with Sesame Oil

Three-Bean Skillet Salad

Tropical Candied Carrots

Pan-Fried Corn Off the Cob

Braised Fennel

Chinese Gingered Eggplant in Garlic Sauce

Skillet Ratatouille

Morels in Pastry Shells with Brandy and Cream

Hashed Sweet Potatoes with Orange Peel and Pecans

Jade Spinach

Indian Summer Squash with Onion and Stewed Tomatoes

Too Many Tomatoes and Sweet Sausage Tomato Sauce

Southwestern Red Beans and Rice

Rice is almost infinitely adaptable, and when cooked in the pan you have plenty of room to add lots of other tasty ingredients. This easy dish goes particularly well with barbecued or broiled flank steak, sausage, and chicken.

2 tablespoons olive oil
1 large onion, chopped
1 celery rib, chopped
1 medium green bell pepper, chopped
1 large garlic clove, minced
1 cup long-grain white rice
1 teaspoon chili powder
½ teaspoon ground cumin
½ teaspoon salt
¼ teaspoon hot pepper sauce, or more to taste
2 cans (14½ ounces each) reduced-sodium chicken broth
1 can (16 ounces) red kidney beans, rinsed and drained

1. In your nonstick frying pan, heat the olive oil over medium-high heat. Add the onion, celery, bell pepper, and garlic. Cook, stirring occasionally, until soft, 5 to 6 minutes.

2. Add the rice, chili powder, cumin, salt, and hot sauce. Cook, stirring, for 1 minute. Pour in the chicken broth and bring to a boil. Cover, reduce the heat to medium-low, and cook until the rice is tender and the liquid is absorbed, 18 to 20 minutes.

3. Stir in the kidney beans and cook until the beans are hot, about 1 minute. Season with additional salt and hot sauce to taste before serving.

SERVES 4 TO 6

HASH BROWN POTATOES WITH ONIONS AND PEPPERS

Hash browns are easiest made with precooked potatoes. That's probably what they grew out of—a need to use up leftovers. It happens upon occasion, though, that we wake up craving eggs and hash browns, and there are no cooked potatoes in the house. It's one of the best times to turn to a microwave. Alternatively, boil the potatoes in their skins until just barely done, then peel.

2 partially cooked and peeled large baking potatoes (about 1¼ pounds),
**   preferably chilled overnight**
1 medium onion, finely chopped
½ cup finely diced bell pepper, green, red, or a mix of both
1 teaspoon coarse salt
½ teaspoon freshly ground pepper
3 tablespoons olive oil

1. Either shred the potatoes on the large holes of a hand grater or in a food processor or finely dice them. Put them in a large bowl.

2. Add the onion, bell pepper, salt, ground pepper, and 1 tablespoon of the olive oil to the potatoes. Toss lightly with 2 forks to mix the ingredients and distribute the oil evenly.

3. Heat your nonstick frying pan over medium-high heat for about 1 minute. Add the remaining olive oil to the pan and heat for 30 seconds longer. Add the potato mixture. With a wide spatula, spread it out to cover the bottom of the pan and press gently to flatten. Cover and cook until the bottom is crusty brown, 3 to 5 minutes.

4. Flip the potatoes over as best you can. It doesn't matter if they break. Just keep turning until most of the browned part is on top. Cover again and cook without disturbing until the bottom is browned again, 2 to 3 minutes. Continue to cook the potatoes, uncovered, breaking them up and flipping them in sections, until they are about half crusty bits and the onion tastes cooked, about 3 minutes longer.

SERVES 3 OR 4

ROQUEFORT POTATO CAKES WITH BROWNED ONIONS

Everyone loves mashed potatoes, but I think if you offer another recipe for them, it should be a little different. A final sautéing in the pan with all kinds of savory goodies is what makes these so special, but I like to boil the potatoes in the pan as well for two reasons: that way when you're done, there's only one pan to clean up; and given the side surface area in direct contact with the heat, the potatoes cook quickly and evenly in the frying pan.

2 large russet (baking) potatoes, preferably Idahos (about 12 ounces each)
1 small onion, finely chopped
3½ tablespoons olive oil
3 tablespoons unsalted butter, melted
1 teaspoon coarse salt
¼ teaspoon freshly ground pepper
⅛ teaspoon cayenne
⅓ cup crumbled Roquefort or other blue cheese

1. A day ahead if you think of it, boil the whole potatoes in a large pot of water for 20 minutes; they will be only partially cooked. Drain and rinse under cold running water to cool. Peel off the skins. Let cool completely. If you have the time, wrap in plastic and refrigerate several hours or overnight. Shred the potatoes in a food processor or on the large holes of a hand grater.

2. Put the chopped onion in your nonstick frying pan along with 1½ tablespoons of the olive oil, cover, and cook over medium heat for 3 minutes, or until sizzling and slightly softened. Uncover and continue to cook, stirring often and reducing the heat slightly if necessary, until the onion is a rich golden brown, about 5 minutes longer. Scrape the browned onion into a large bowl.

3. Add the shredded potatoes and the melted butter. Sprinkle on the salt, pepper, and cayenne and toss to mix well. With your hands, form half the potato mixture into 4 flat cakes about 4 inches in diameter. Sprinkle one-quarter of the crumbled Roquefort over each cake, leaving a small margin around the rim. Form 4 more cakes from the remaining potato mixture. As you shape each cake, set it on top of 1 of the cheese-covered cakes and press together around the edges to sandwich the cheese in the middle. Tamp the edges to form a neat potato cake.

4. In your pan, heat the remaining 2 tablespoons olive oil over medium heat. Add the potato cakes, press down gently with a wide spatula, cover, and cook until browned on the bottom, 4 to 5 minutes. Carefully turn the cakes over with a wide spatula and cook, still covered, until the second side is browned and the potatoes are tender, 4 to 5 minutes longer. If the cakes start cooking too fast, reduce the heat slightly. Serve at once or set aside and reheat in a hot oven at mealtime.

SERVES 4

POTATO, CARROT, AND CELERY ROOT PANCAKES

The addition of sweet carrots and pungent celery root (also called celeriac) creates deeply flavorful potato pancakes better known as latkes, one that tastes particularly fine alongside crisp roast chicken or tender braised brisket. Top these with sour cream, if desired. But to me, due to the carrots and celery root, they seem even more compatible with that other latke-friendly topping: homemade applesauce.

2 medium russet (baking) potatoes (about 1 pound), peeled
2 large carrots (about ½ pound), peeled
⅓ cup shredded peeled celery root
1¼ teaspoons salt
2 eggs
2 tablespoons flour
2 scallions, thinly sliced
½ teaspoon freshly ground pepper
About ⅓ cup peanut oil or melted butter

1. Preheat the oven to 200 degrees F. Line 2 sheet pans with several thicknesses of paper towels.

2. Set a colander in the sink. Using the coarse holes of a standard box grater, shred the potatoes and carrots into the colander. Add the celery root and salt, toss, and let stand, stirring occasionally, for 15 minutes.

3. Meanwhile, in a large bowl, whisk together the eggs, flour, scallions, and pepper.

4. Squeeze the potato mixture firmly in your hands and press against the colander to expel as much liquid as possible. Add the vegetables to the egg mixture in the bowl. Stir well.

5. Set your nonstick frying pan over medium heat. When it is hot, add 2 tablespoons of the oil. Working in batches, scoop 2 rounded tablespoons of the potato mixture at a time into the oil. Flatten slightly and cook, turning once, until crisp and golden brown, 6 to 8 minutes total. Transfer the browned latkes to the prepared sheet pans and keep them warm in the oven while cooking the remaining latkes, adding more oil to the pan as needed. Serve immediately.

SERVES 4 TO 6

Buttermilk-Scallion Hush Puppies

Said to have been originally tossed to dogs at Southern fish fries to stop their hungry whining, these little fritters are the best possible accompaniment to the catfish on page 102 (and way too good for the collie). For maximum efficiency, cook the hush puppies first and keep them warm in the oven, while you fry the catfish in the same pan in fresh oil.

1 egg
¾ cup buttermilk, at room temperature
4 cups plus 2 tablespoons peanut oil
2 scallions, thinly sliced
1½ cups yellow cornmeal
½ cup flour
1 tablespoon sugar
1 tablespoon baking powder
¼ teaspoon baking soda
¾ teaspoon salt

1. Preheat the oven to 250 degrees F. In a small bowl, beat the egg lightly. Whisk in the buttermilk, 2 tablespoons of the oil, and the scallions.

2. In a large bowl, stir together the cornmeal, flour, sugar, baking powder, baking soda, and salt. Add the buttermilk mixture and stir to combine; the dough will be stiff.

3. Meanwhile, in your nonstick frying pan, heat the remaining 4 cups oil until hot but not smoking. Working in 2 or 3 batches, with a spoon, scoop up small portions of the dough and shape them into 1-inch balls. Carefully lower the

balls into the hot fat and fry over medium heat, turning once, until golden brown and just cooked through, about 2 minutes. With a slotted spoon, transfer to a sheet pan lined with paper towels and keep warm in the oven until all are fried. Serve hot.

SERVES 4 TO 6

CHEESY POLENTA IN THE PAN

If you haven't tasted it, know that polenta is the Italian equivalent of our Southern grits. While the cornmeal can end up with a variety of textures, this one is soft and creamy. It goes well with roast chicken, pork, ham, and sausages and peppers.

The pan is perfect for cooking polenta, allowing lots of surface area for evaporation of the liquid. The only trick is to avoid lumps. The best way to accomplish this is to dissolve the cornmeal is some cold water first, then stir the slurry into a pan of boiling water. For convenience, I used ordinary stone-ground yellow cornmeal. If you have access to instant Italian polenta, by all means use it; it will cook in half the time. (Non-instant polenta, by contrast, takes 30 to 45 minutes.)

1 cup stone-ground yellow cornmeal
1 teaspoon salt
Dash of cayenne
2 tablespoons butter
¾ cup shredded Italian fontina or Monterey Jack cheese
¼ cup freshly grated Parmesan cheese

1. In your nonstick frying pan, bring 3 cups water to a boil over high heat. Meanwhile, put the cornmeal in a medium bowl. Stir in 1½ cups cold water until the cornmeal is all loose and blended with no lumps.

2. When the water boils, add the salt and cayenne. Slowly stir in the cornmeal slurry until it is all added and evenly blended. Immediately reduce the heat to low. Cook, stirring often, for 10 minutes.

3. Raise the heat to medium-low and continue to cook, stirring constantly, until the mixture thickens and the mass begins to pull away from the sides of the pan, about 5 minutes longer.

4. Add the butter. Stir in the fontina and Parmesan cheeses until melted and smooth. Season the polenta with additional salt to taste and serve at once.

SERVES 4 TO 6

SAUTÉED ARTICHOKE HEARTS WITH MELTED FONTINA CHEESE

I'm sorry, but I'm afraid artichoke hearts win the award for "Canned Vegetable Least Likely to Taste Like Itself." So even though it's a pain, you're going to have to use fresh. Artichokes usually go on sale twice a year—in late spring and early fall.

2 large or 3 medium artichokes
1 tablespoon butter
2 tablespoons olive oil
1 pound white or cremini mushrooms, chopped
¼ pound grated Fontina cheese (about 1 cup)

1. Cut the top third off the artichokes, remove the tough outer leaves, and cut off the stems ½ inch from the base. Cut each artichoke in half. Fill your nonstick frying pan half full with water, add the artichoke halves cut sides down, cover, and boil for 10 minutes; drain. When the artichokes are cool enough to handle, remove the remaining leaves. With a paring knife or the edge of a spoon, remove all of the fuzzy "choke" at the artichokes' centers. Slice the hearts into bite-size pieces and set aside.

2. Wipe the pan dry. Add the butter and olive oil and set over high heat. Add the mushrooms and sauté, stirring frequently, until tender, about 5 minutes. Add the artichoke hearts and continue sautéing until the mushrooms turn brown, another 3 to 4 minutes.

3. Reduce the heat to medium. Sprinkle the cheese over the artichokes and mushrooms. Cover and cook until melted, 1 to 2 minutes. Transfer to a warm serving dish.

Variation: To turn this into a great one-pan meal, add 4 to 5 ounces of diced ham or coarsely crumbled cooked bacon and maybe a cut-up green pepper in the middle of step 2. Stir in a cup (roughly half a 14-ounce can) of stewed tomatoes after the cheese melts and heat through.

SERVES 4

Stir-Fried Asparagus with Sesame Oil

With asparagus in season, the simplest recipe is usually the best. But we eat so much of it, I'm always looking for an alternative to steaming or roasting. Here's a great way to cook asparagus in the pan, which seems to intensify its flavor and natural sweetness. Don't forget, like corn on the cob, asparagus is sweetest as soon as it is picked, so try to cook it the day you buy it.

1 pound fresh asparagus
2 tablespoons peanut or olive oil
1 teaspoon sugar
½ teaspoon salt
1½ teaspoons Asian sesame oil

1. Trim the tough ends off the asparagus. Cut the stalks crosswise on an angle into ¾- to 1-inch pieces. Keep the tips and tender part of the stalks separate from the thicker ends.

2. Heat your nonstick frying pan over high heat for about 30 seconds. Add the peanut oil and heat for 30 seconds longer. Add the thicker pieces of asparagus first. Sprinkle on the sugar and salt and sauté about 1 minute longer, until some pieces are lightly browned in spots.

3. Pour ½ cup water into the pan, cover, and continue to cook over high heat for 1 to 2 minutes, until the asparagus is just barely tender. Uncover and boil until almost all the liquid evaporates. Drizzle the sesame oil over the asparagus, toss, and serve.

SERVES 3 OR 4

TROPICAL CANDIED CARROTS

Just a hint of exotic fruit along with a double dose of ginger turns everyday carrots into a sweet treat even the kids will love. Given that carrots are loaded with vitamin A, that they keep in the fridge for weeks, and that they go with everything from chicken to fish, this is one of my favorite vegetable dishes.

1 pound carrots, peeled and sliced
1 cup mango or passionfruit nectar
1½ tablespoons unsalted butter
2 tablespoons dark brown sugar
¾ teaspoon powdered ginger
1 to 2 tablespoons minced crystallized ginger (optional)

1. Place the carrots in your nonstick frying pan along with the passionfruit nectar, butter, brown sugar, and powdered ginger. Bring the liquid to a boil. Reduce the heat to medium, cover the pan, and cook until the carrots are just barely tender, about 5 minutes.

2. Uncover, raise the heat to medium-high, and cook, stirring, until the carrots are tender and the liquid in the pan is reduced to a glaze, 5 to 7 minutes longer. Stir in the crystallized ginger if you have it and serve.

SERVES 4 TO 6

Three-Bean Skillet Salad

Growing up in Memphis, certain country-style dishes still resonate with me. Bean salads were a staple at all our barbecues, family get-togethers, and picnics. There's little room to improve on the old-fashioned sweet-sour, colorful multi-bean mixtures, part salad, part pickle, which go so well with everything from barbecued chicken to hamburgers, providing a spicy foil to creamy potato or macaroni salad. I have updated the salad a bit, though, by using fresh beans. In the pan, this recipe is simple, quick, and quintessentially American. One note: While the salad is best marinated overnight, the vinegar will cause the green beans to lose their color over time.

¾ **pound yellow wax beans***
¾ **pound green beans**
¾ **cup cider vinegar**
¾ **cup water**
⅓ **cup sugar**
¾ **teaspoon salt**
1 **teaspoon whole black peppercorns**
1 **teaspoon allspice berries**
3 **whole cloves**
2 **cinnamon sticks**
1 **medium white onion, quartered lengthwise and sliced**
3 **tablespoons vegetable oil or olive oil**
1 **can (15 ounces) red kidney beans, rinsed and drained**

1. Keeping them separate, trim the ends off both the wax beans and the green beans. Cut them into halves or thirds so the pieces are about 1 inch long.

2. Fill your nonstick frying pan halfway with salted water and bring to a boil. Add the wax beans and cook until just crisp-tender, 3 to 5 minutes. Remove with a slotted skimmer or large spoon and rinse under cold running water; drain

well. Add the green beans to the pan and cook until just crisp-tender, 3 to 5 minutes. Drain and rinse under cold running water; drain well.

3. In the pan, combine the vinegar, water, sugar, salt, peppercorns, allspice berries, cloves, and cinnamon sticks. Bring to a boil, stirring to dissolve the sugar. Reduce the heat to low and let the syrup steep for 10 minutes. Strain to remove the whole spices and return the syrup to the pan.

4. Add the wax beans, green beans, and onion to the syrup. Bring to a boil, reduce the heat to a simmer, cover, and cook for 5 minutes. Stir occasionally so the onions soften evenly. Remove from the heat. Let stand until cool.

5. Transfer to a covered container, drizzle the olive oil over the top, and refrigerate overnight. Transfer to a large serving bowl and stir in the beans. Serve slightly chilled or at room temperature, using a slotted spoon to lift the beans from the dressing.

* Green beans are available year-round, but wax beans are sometimes hard to find. If fresh are not available, use a 15-ounce can, drained and well rinsed. Add them in step 4.

SERVES 6 TO 8

Pan-Fried Corn Off the Cob

Full of color and brightly flavored, this quick side dish goes well with grilled meats and chicken and with any Mexican food. If you're making it in corn season, just throw fresh ears in the microwave for a minute or two until barely tender before cutting the kernels off the cob.

1 teaspoon cumin seeds
2 tablespoons corn or peanut oil
1 small onion, chopped
3 garlic cloves, finely chopped
½ medium green bell pepper, diced
½ red bell pepper, diced
1 jalapeño pepper, seeded and minced
3 cups corn kernels—cooked fresh, frozen, or canned
Juice of 1 lime
1 teaspoon sugar
Salt and freshly ground pepper

1. Place the cumin seeds in your nonstick frying pan. Set over medium heat and cook, shaking the pan, until the seeds are lightly browned and fragrant, 2 to 3 minutes. Pour into a small dish.

2. Heat the oil in the pan over medium-high heat. Add the onion and cook until softened, 2 to 3 minutes. Add the garlic, green and red bell peppers, and jalapeño and sauté until the peppers are softened but still bright colored, about 2 minutes.

3. Add the corn, raise the heat to high, and cook, stirring, until heated through and just beginning to brown, 3 to 5 minutes. Sprinkle on the lime juice and sugar. Cook, stirring, 1 minute longer. Season with salt and pepper to taste and serve.

SERVES 4 TO 6

BRAISED FENNEL

Only in recent years has this Italian staple become readily available in supermarket produce departments. It looks like overgrown celery with a big white bulb at the bottom and hairy green fronds growing off the top. Only the bulb is eaten; the green stalks are too tough. Raw fennel tastes like celery with a licorice twist—crisp, clean, and refreshing. In fact, it's sometimes labeled "anise." Cooked, the vegetable becomes transformed, turning sweet and nutty, with a mild flavor not unlike that of artichokes. Braised fennel goes especially well with roast pork and chicken.

2 bulbs fresh fennel
3 tablespoons olive oil
1 garlic clove, minced
¼ teaspoon dried thyme leaves
¼ teaspoon salt
¼ teaspoon freshly ground pepper
1 cup chicken broth or water

1. Trim a thin slice off the root end of the bulbs. Cut the green stalks off the top. Cut each fennel bulb lengthwise into 4 slices ⅜ to ½ inch thick.

2. In your nonstick frying pan, heat the olive oil over medium-high heat. Add the fennel slices in batches so they lie flat and cook until golden brown on the bottom, 3 to 5 minutes. Turn over and cook until golden brown on the second side, about 3 minutes. Remove with a slotted spatula while you sauté the remaining fennel.

3. Return all the fennel to the pan. Season with the garlic, thyme, salt, and pepper. Pour in the stock and bring to a boil. Reduce the heat to medium-low, cover, and cook until the fennel is tender but not mushy, about 10 minutes. Turn the pieces over about halfway through and bring the bottom ones to the top and vice versa so they cook evenly. If there is liquid left in the pan, raise the heat and cook, uncovered, until all but a few tablespoons evaporates.

SERVES 4 TO 6

Chinese Gingered Eggplant in Garlic Sauce

With its large surface area, the pan is perfect for stir-frying. Since compared to a wok the sides are low, you just have to be a little more careful to keep everything inside the pan. One solution is to cook the ingredients in two batches.

When choosing eggplants, look for firm vegetables with tight, shiny skins. The tops should be green and fresh looking, not brown and shriveled. If you have access to the long narrow Asian eggplants, they are best for this dish. Otherwise, choose the smallest Italian eggplants you can find.

1½ to 2 pounds eggplants
⅓ cup chicken broth or water
2 tablespoons soy sauce
2 tablespoons brown sugar
1 tablespoon cider vinegar
1 tablespoon dry sherry
¾ teaspoon cornstarch
⅓ cup peanut oil
1 tablespoon minced fresh ginger
2 teaspoons minced garlic
¼ teaspoon crushed hot pepper flakes
1 teaspoon Asian sesame oil

1. Trim the ends from the eggplants; peel them if you prefer. Cut the eggplants into ¾-inch dice.

2. In a small bowl, combine the broth, soy sauce, brown sugar, vinegar, sherry, and cornstarch. Stir to dissolve the sugar and cornstarch. Set the sauce aside.

3. Heat 2 tablespoons of the peanut oil in the pan over medium-high heat. Add half of the eggplant and cook, turning with a wide spatula, until golden

brown and tender, 5 to 7 minutes. Remove to a plate. Repeat with another 2 tablespoons peanut oil and the remaining eggplant. Remove to the plate.

4. Reduce the heat to medium. Heat the remaining 1 tablespoon peanut oil in the pan. Add the ginger and garlic and sauté for 30 to 60 seconds, until fragrant but not browned. Add the hot pepper. Give the sauce a quick stir and immediately pour it into the pan. Bring to a boil, stirring constantly, until thickened.

5. Return the eggplant to the pan and cook, stirring gently to coat with sauce, about 1 minute. Remove from the heat, stir in the sesame oil, and serve.

SERVES 4

Skillet Ratatouille

Commonly called a stew, ratatouille is made up of assorted vegetables that require thorough browning if the dish is to taste its best—perfect work for the pan. Undercook the ratatouille for a more al dente texture or simmer it longer to create a near-puree: It's cook's choice. Served hot or cold, the dish is particularly good beside lamb, and works well with beef, chicken, and hearty fish, too.

3 tablespoons olive oil
1 medium eggplant (about 1 pound), cut into ¾-inch cubes
Salt
3 small zucchini (about 12 ounces total), trimmed and cut into ¾-inch pieces
2 medium red bell peppers, cut into ¾-inch pieces
1 medium onion, halved and thinly sliced
1 teaspoon dried basil
4 garlic cloves, finely chopped
2 cups seeded, chopped ripe plum tomatoes (from about 5 medium)
½ cup canned crushed tomatoes with added puree
1 bay leaf
Freshly ground black pepper

1. Set your nonstick frying pan over medium heat. Add 2 teaspoons of the oil and when it is hot, add half the eggplant. Toss immediately to coat with oil, sprinkle with a pinch of salt, and cook, stirring occasionally, until browned, about 7 minutes. Transfer the eggplant to a bowl. Heat another 2 teaspoons oil in the pan and repeat with the remaining eggplant.

2. Add 2 teaspoons oil to the pan and set over medium heat. Add the zucchini, season with a pinch of salt, and cook, stirring occasionally, until browned, about 7 minutes. Transfer to the bowl with the eggplant.

3. Add the remaining 1 tablespoon oil to the pan. Add the bell peppers, onion, and basil. Cook, stirring occasionally, until the onion is lightly browned, about 5 minutes. Add the garlic and cook, stirring often, for 3 minutes. Stir in the fresh and canned tomatoes, bay leaf, and ½ teaspoon salt. Return the eggplant and zucchini to the pan. Season generously with pepper.

4. Cover, reduce the heat to medium-low, and simmer, stirring once or twice, until juicy, about 20 minutes. Uncover and cook, stirring often, until the ratatouille is done to your liking, about 10 minutes for a slightly al dente result, 25 minutes for a softer texture. Season with additional salt and pepper to taste.

5. If possible, cover the ratatouille and let it sit overnight in the refrigerator. Use at room temperature or reheat before serving.

SERVES 6

MORELS IN PASTRY SHELLS WITH BRANDY AND CREAM

Morel mushrooms are among the royalty of the fungi kingdom. Their unique, smoky flavor makes them one of the most desirable food items in the world. Fresh morels are available in most gourmet groceries in the spring. They're expensive, so the idea is to use as few as possible in recipes that extend their taste.

These luscious pastry shells make a knockout elegant first course. Or they can be served as a side dish along with a standing rib roast, chicken, or game hens.

4 frozen individual puff pastry shells
1 tablespoon unsalted butter
1 tablespoon olive oil
1 small sweet onion, such as Vidalia, finely chopped
1 small red bell pepper, finely chopped
8 ounces fresh morels, finely chopped
1 cup fresh basil, finely chopped
1 teaspoon sugar
2 tablespoons brandy
½ cup heavy cream

1. Bake the puff pastries in the oven as directed by the package instructions.

2. While the pastries are baking, in your nonstick frying pan, melt the butter in the oil over medium-high heat. Add the onion and red bell pepper and sauté until the onion is softened and translucent, 2 to 3 minutes.

3. Add the morels, basil, and sugar and sauté until the morels give up their liquid and it evaporates, 6 to 8 minutes.

4. Raise the heat to high. Add the brandy and flame; carefully ignite with a match if it doesn't just catch. As soon as the flames subside, pour in the cream and boil until the sauce thickens, 2 to 3 minutes.

5. Place the puff pastry shells on separate plates. Fill each with the morel mixture and serve at once.

SERVES 4

HASHED SWEET POTATOES WITH ORANGE PEEL AND PECANS

Not totally ooey-gooey, like the sweet potatoes of Thanksgiving, these are still treat food, and they make a very nice accompaniment to poultry, ham, or pork dishes of all sorts. The sweets will be easier to handle if precooked and chilled overnight, before their final browning and crisping in the pan.

2½ pounds sweet potatoes (3 medium), peeled and cut into large chunks
Salt
½ cup pecans
3 tablespoons unsalted butter
1 tablespoon peanut or canola oil
1 tablespoon minced orange zest
2 tablespoons packed light brown sugar
Freshly ground pepper

1. In a large saucepan, cover the potato chunks with cold water. Add 1 table-spoon salt and set over high heat. Bring to a simmer, then partially cover, lower the heat, and cook for about 25 minutes. The potatoes will not be tender and will still show some resistance at their centers when pierced with a knife. Drain, let cool, and refrigerate at least several hours, overnight if possible. Cut the cold sweet potatoes into ½-inch chunks.

2. Preheat the oven to 375 degrees F. In a shallow metal pan, like a cake tin, toast the pecans, stirring once or twice, until crisp, lightly browned, and fragrant, 8 to 10 minutes. Remove from the pan, let cool, then coarsely chop.

3. In your nonstick frying pan, melt the butter in the oil over medium heat. Add the orange zest and cook, stirring often, for 30 seconds. Add the sweet potatoes and stir to coat with the orange butter mixture. Reduce the heat slightly

and cook, turning the potatoes every few minutes with a spatula, until they are lightly browned and tender, 15 to 20 minutes.

4. Stir in the toasted pecans, brown sugar, ½ teaspoon salt, and ¼ teaspoon pepper. Cook 2 minutes longer and serve.

SERVES 4 TO 6

JADE SPINACH

Convenience counts more than ever these days. Fresh spinach used to be a lot of work to cook, simply because of all the rinsing and trimming. Now many supermarkets carry prepackaged sealed bags of baby spinach all washed and ready to go. That's what I use for this pretty, bright green dish. The wide surface area of the large nonstick pan is great here, because it allows the spinach to wilt quickly so it doesn't overcook.

1 tablespoon peanut or olive oil
1 pound fresh spinach, preferably baby leaves, rinsed and dried
1 teaspoon sugar
¼ teaspoon salt
2 teaspoons soy sauce
1½ teaspoons rice vinegar
1 teaspoon Asian sesame oil

1. Heat your nonstick frying pan for about 1 minute, until hot. Add the oil and let it heat up for about 30 seconds. Gradually add the spinach by handfuls, turning and stirring it with 2 wooden spoons or a salad tongs. As soon as one batch wilts slightly, add another, fitting as much as you can in the pan at one time.

2. When all the spinach has been added, sprinkle on the sugar and salt. Cook, turning and stirring, until the spinach is just barely tender but still bright green, about 1 minute.

3. Toss with the soy sauce, rice vinegar, and sesame oil and remove from the heat. Serve hot, at room temperature, or chilled.

SERVES 2 OR 3

Indian Summer Squash with Onion and Stewed Tomatoes

This simple recipe is a great late-fall, early-winter side dish. Because it is saucy, I particularly like to serve it with rice. To turn the vegetable dish into an instant one-pan meal, just add a can of chickpeas (garbanzo beans) and whatever left-over shredded cooked beef, lamb, or chicken you have on hand.

1 tablespoon unsalted butter
1 tablespoon olive oil
2 medium yellow squash, thinly sliced into rounds
1 large sweet onion, chopped
1 can (14½ ounces) stewed tomatoes
1 teaspoon curry powder

1. In your nonstick frying pan, melt the butter in the olive oil over medium-high heat. Add the squash and onion and cook, stirring frequently, until the squash is just tender, about 5 minutes.

2. Stir in the stewed tomatoes and the curry powder. Bring to a simmer and cook until heated through, about 3 minutes.

SERVES 4

Too Many Tomatoes and Sweet Sausage Tomato Sauce

Every year in early fall, when there's an overabundance of tomatoes at my local market and I can buy them in quantity, slightly bruised, at a bargain price, I make this savory sauce at least once a week. It's a recipe I've also shared with friends who have gardens and end up in late August or September with too many tomatoes all at once. The idea is to freeze the sauce for midwinter nights, when fresh tomatoes are scarce and pricey, but somehow, each batch never seems to make it through to the next weekend.

While this recipe can be made entirely in the pan, assuming you have a model with deep sides, in fact, it's much more practical to use both the pan and a deep pot to avoid splatters. Nonetheless, since it's one of my favorite recipes, I couldn't resist including it in this book.

5 pounds large fresh tomatoes, peeled* and finely chopped
1 can (6 ounces) tomato paste (optional)
2 tablespoons balsamic vinegar
1 tablespoon Worcestershire sauce
1½ teaspoons salt
½ teaspoon freshly ground pepper
1 tablespoon olive oil
4 sweet Italian sausages (about 1 pound)
1 large sweet onion, chopped
1 large green bell pepper, chopped
4 garlic cloves, minced
1 cup finely chopped fresh basil

1. Place the tomatoes in a large nonreactive stockpot or Dutch oven. Bring to a boil over medium-high heat. Cover, reduce the heat to medium, and cook for 10 minutes. Remove the cover and cook, stirring often, for 10 minutes longer.

2. If you like a thicker sauce, stir in the tomato paste. Stir in the balsamic vinegar, Worcestershire sauce, salt, and pepper. Remove from the heat and set the tomato sauce aside.

3. In your nonstick frying pan, heat the olive oil over high heat. Add the sausages, onion, and bell pepper. Cook, stirring, until the sausage is lightly browned, about 5 minutes. Add the garlic and cook for 1 minute. Reduce the heat to medium. Add the basil, mix well, and simmer for 2 minutes.

4. Scrape everything from the pan into the tomato sauce. Bring to a boil, reduce the heat to low, cover, and simmer for 20 minutes. Season with additional salt and pepper to taste before using.

* To peel tomatoes easily, drop them in a pot of boiling water for 10 to 20 seconds. Remove and the skins will slip right off.

MAKES ABOUT 2 QUARTS

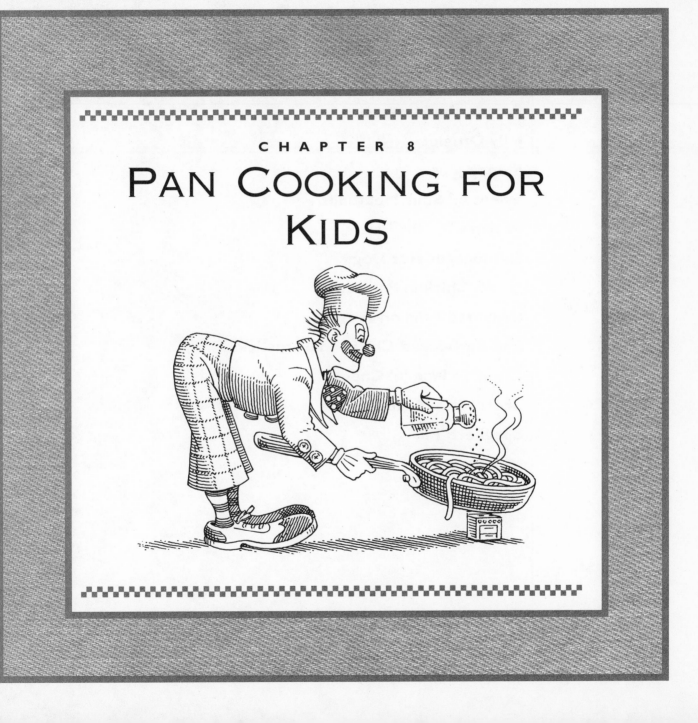

CHAPTER 8
PAN COOKING FOR KIDS

Salsa and Cheese Omelet

Buttermilk Flapjacks

Frog in the Haystack

Jelly Omelet

Sloppy Joes

Sweet 'n' Sour Meatballs

Jordan's Tortilla Pizza

Hamburger Hot Dogs

Quick Chicken Parmesan

Creamed Tuna on Toast

Pan-Barbecued Chicken Drumsticks

One-Pan Mac 'n' Cheese

Shells with Meat Sauce

Spaghetti Pie

Salsa and Cheese Omelet

Children like their eggs firm and their cheese runny, so this quick egg dish is pretty well assured of popularity with the younger set. A thin folded omelet that fits the pan will feed two, but since it takes about two minutes to make, you can easily do a repeat performance. I call for mild salsa, but some kids enjoy a lot of heat; if yours do, by all means substitute a spicier variety. Serve with toast or warm corn tortillas.

4 eggs
1 tablespoon water
½ teaspoon salt
¼ teaspoon freshly ground pepper
2 tablespoons butter
4 slices of American cheese
3 to 4 tablespoons mild tomato salsa

1. Beat the eggs with the water, salt, and pepper. When the mixture hits the hot pan, the water turns into steam, creating a light, fluffy omelet.

2. Melt the butter in your nonstick frying pan over medium-high heat. Wait until the foam from the butter subsides. Then pour in the eggs all at once and tilt and swirl the pan to help the eggs cover the bottom evenly. With a wide spatula, lift the edge of the omelet and tilt again to let any loose egg run underneath. Reduce the heat to medium-low and cook about 1 minute, until the egg is just barely set on top.

3. Arrange the American cheese on top of the eggs. Cover the pan and cook 30 to 60 seconds, until the cheese is melted. Immediately fold the omelet in half or roll it into thirds as you slide it onto a platter. Spoon the salsa over the top and cut in half to serve.

SERVES 2

Buttermilk Flapjacks

Drama is something kids really enjoy. So if it's a weekend morning and you're trying to entertain your children while you feed them, this is a great recipe to choose. And the nonstick pan will make you look better than you probably are as a short-order chef. Just remember, it's all in the wrist. P.S.: If your flapjacks don't flip the way you'd like, there's no shame in resorting to a spatula. Just don't let your children see you do it.

**1 cup flour
1 tablespoon sugar
1 teaspoon baking powder
½ teaspoon baking soda
¼ teaspoon salt
1 egg
1 cup buttermilk
2 tablespoons melted butter or vegetable oil**

1. Sift the flour, sugar, baking powder, baking soda, and salt together into a mixing bowl.

2. In a 2-cup glass measure or small bowl, beat the egg lightly. Whisk in the buttermilk and melted butter or oil until well blended.

3. Stir the wet ingredients into the dry, mixing only until the batter is evenly moistened; it will still contain small lumps.

4. Grease your nonstick frying pan lightly with a paper towel moistened with vegetable oil. Heat over medium heat for about 1 minute. Ladle ⅓ cup of the batter into the pan. Spread out to 6 or 7 inches. Cook until golden brown on the bottom with tiny bubbles all over the top, 1½ to 2 minutes.

5. Shake the pan or slip a spatula underneath the flapjack to loosen it. Then take a deep breath, jerk the pan up and away from you, flipping the pancake and letting it slide back into the pan, browned side up. Good luck! You'll find this takes some practice and a certain amount of trial and error. When you get it right, repeat with the remaining batter. Serve the flapjacks hot out of the pan.

SERVES 3 OR 4

Frog in the Haystack

My version of Toad in the Hole, a traditional British kids' dish made of sausages buried in a sort of Yorkshire pudding batter, then baked in the oven. This all-American pan interpretation hides chunks of browned sausage inside corn fritter batter. Since the children are usually hungry in the morning and all want to eat at once and since the batter is best cooked up as soon as it is assembled, cook the batter all at once. Just cut into wedges to serve. Pass syrup on the side. And don't forget to ask the kids what part of the frog they're chewing on now.

½ **package brown-and-serve sausages (about ½ pound)**
1 can (11 ounces) vacuum-packed corn niblets
3 eggs, separated
⅓ **cup flour**
1 teaspoon sugar
½ **teaspoon baking powder**
¼ **teaspoon salt**
3 tablespoons butter

1. In your nonstick frying pan, brown the sausages as directed on the package. Drain the sausages on paper towels. When they are cool, transfer to a cutting board and slice them into ½- to ¾-inch chunks. Rinse and wipe out the pan.

2. Drain the corn and dump it into a food processor. Pulse until most of the kernels are chopped.

3. In a medium bowl, with an electric hand mixer, beat the egg whites until they form soft peaks.

4. In a large bowl, beat the egg yolks well. Mix in the flour, sugar, baking powder, and salt. Stir in the corn. Add the egg whites and fold just until no streaks of white remain.

5. Melt 2 tablespoons of the butter in the pan over medium-high heat. Pour in the batter and reduce the heat to medium-low. Cook for 1 minute to allow the batter to set on the bottom. Distribute the sausage chunks evenly around the batter. Cover the pan and cook until the "haystack" is mostly set, puffed around the edges, and golden brown on the bottom but still loose in the center, 3 to 4 minutes.

6. Loosen the giant corn fritter with a spatula and slide it out onto the lid or a large round platter. Melt the remaining 1 tablespoon butter in the pan. Carefully invert the fritter back into the pan and cook until puffed and firm throughout and lightly browned on the second side, about 3 minutes longer. Serve at once.

SERVES 4 TO 6 KIDS

Jelly Omelet

If your kids are fans of Dr. Seuss's *Green Eggs and Ham,* this is the dish for them. The blue in the jelly mixes with the egg to tinge parts of it a color that would only appeal to a child. This dish is modeled after just such an omelet I once ordered as a very young person at the Serendipity restaurant in New York City.

3 eggs
1 tablespoon milk or water
Salt and freshly ground pepper
2 tablespoons butter
3 tablespoons grape jelly or seedless raspberry jam

1. In a small bowl, beat the eggs with the milk until blended. Season lightly with salt and pepper.

2. Melt the butter in your nonstick frying pan over high heat. As soon as the foam subsides, pour in the eggs and reduce the heat to medium. Cook, swirling and lifting the omelet so the uncooked portion runs underneath, until mostly set but still soft and shiny on top, about 2 minutes.

3. Spread or dollop the jelly down the center and smooth it over the omelet as evenly as you can. Roll up the omelet like a jelly roll and cook 30 seconds longer. Cut the omelet in half on an angle like a wrap sandwich, so as much of the jelly spiral shows as possible, and transfer to plates. Serve at once.

SERVES 2

Sloppy Joes

Sloppy Joes relax the rules and let kids and parents alike know it's okay to be just a little messy at the table. This recipe makes a skilletful, which will feed a crowd or provide several smaller, almost instant meals throughout a busy week.

1 tablespoon olive or canola oil
1½ cups finely chopped onion
1 teaspoon chili powder
2 pounds lean ground beef
1 teaspoon salt
¾ cup ketchup
¾ cup canned beef broth
1 can (10¾ ounces) condensed tomato soup
1 tablespoon Worcestershire sauce
½ teaspoon freshly ground pepper
8 large premium hamburger buns or sandwich rolls

1. In your nonstick frying pan, warm the oil over medium heat. Add the onion and chili powder, cover, and cook, stirring once or twice, for 10 minutes. Crumble the beef into the pan, season with the salt, and cook, uncovered, breaking up the lumps, until no longer pink, about 10 minutes. Add the ketchup, broth, soup, Worcestershire sauce, and pepper and bring to a simmer. Partially cover the pan, lower the heat slightly, and cook, stirring occasionally, until thick, 30 to 40 minutes. The meat mixture can be prepared up to 3 days ahead. Refrigerate, covered, and reheat in the pan just before serving.

2. Toast the hamburger buns lightly, if desired. Ladle a generous spoonful of the meat mixture over the bun. It should spill over onto the plate; do not expect the bun to contain it all. Set the bun top in place and serve immediately. Provide lots of paper napkins.

MAKES 8 MESSY SANDWICHES

Sweet 'n' Sour Meatballs

One man's retro appetizer is another child's scrumptious main course. Serve over spaghetti, rice, or on a hot dog bun.

1 egg
2 tablespoons milk
1 pound ground beef
1 cup soft bread crumbs
1 teaspoon salt
⅛ teaspoon freshly ground pepper
2 tablespoons vegetable oil
1 cup chili sauce
1 cup red currant jelly

1. In a medium bowl, beat together the egg and milk. Add the beef, bread crumbs, salt, and pepper. Mix very well—I use my hands—until thoroughly combined. Form into 20 to 25 spoon-sized meatballs.

2. Heat the oil in your nonstick frying pan over high heat. Add the meatballs and cook, turning, until lightly browned, about 5 minutes.

3. Add the chili sauce and jelly. Stir until the jelly is melted. Reduce the heat, cover, and simmer 10 to 12 minutes, until the sauce thickens.

SERVES 4

Jordan's Tortilla Pizza

Jordan Sims' mom, Abby, keeps small containers of homemade tomato sauce in the freezer so that her two sons can make a meal for themselves whenever the hunger pangs hit. This is 11-year-old Jordan's favorite recipe.

4 tablespoons butter
4 large flour tortillas, 10 inches in diameter
½ cup homemade tomato sauce or canned tomato or taco sauce
1 cup shredded mozzarella cheese

1. Melt 1 tablespoon of the butter in your nonstick frying pan over medium-high heat. Place 1 tortilla in the pan and cook until slightly browned underneath, about 2 minutes.

2. Turn over the tortilla and spread 2 tablespoons of tomato sauce over half of the tortilla using the back of a spoon to smooth out the sauce. Sprinkle ¼ cup cheese over the tomato sauce. Fold the uncovered half of the tortilla over the top of the sauce and cheese to form a semicircle. Cover the pan and cook for 2 minutes. Remove the tortilla from the pan and serve.

3. Repeat the above 3 more times.

SERVES 4

Hamburger Hot Dogs

Imagination adds a lot of fun to food. One good way to get kids to eat their second favorite food—hamburgers—is to make it look like their all-time favorite food—hot dogs. Here's my way to slip them some lean meat and have a good time making lunch. As an alternative to hot dog buns, the "dogs" can be rolled up in lettuce leaves or flour tortillas smeared with ketchup or salsa. Pass potato chips, carrot sticks, and sweet pickle slices on the side.

I pound lean ground beef, such as ground round
I tablespoon ketchup
I teaspoon Dijon or yellow mustard
I teaspoon paprika
½ teaspoon garlic powder
½ teaspoon salt
¼ teaspoon freshly ground pepper
Split hot dog buns, ketchup and mustard (preferably in squeeze bottles), and
**   pickle relish, for serving**

1. Put the ground beef in a bowl. Add the ketchup, mustard, paprika, garlic powder, salt, and pepper. Using your hands, mix lightly but well until the ingredients are evenly combined. (Depending upon their sensibilities, one or more of your kids might want to help with this or with forming the "hot dogs" in the next step.)

2. Divide the seasoned beef into 8 equal parts. On a clean countertop or on a sheet of waxed paper, roll each part under your palms into a 5½- to 6-inch log about ¾ inch in diameter and the shape of a hot dog.

3. Heat your nonstick frying pan over medium-high heat for 30 to 60 seconds. Add the dogs and cook, turning, to sear the outsides for about 1 minute. Reduce the heat to medium-low and continue to cook, turning the hot dogs as they

brown, until they are no longer pink inside but are still juicy, about 6 minutes longer. If they start to brown too much before they are cooked through, add a few tablespoons of water to the pan. Sandwich inside the buns and pass the ketchup, mustard, and relish on the side.

SERVES 4 TO 6

QUICK CHICKEN PARMESAN

Here's another kid-pleaser that can be thrown together quickly in the pan. And to tell the truth, my wife and I enjoy this as well. We like to start with a tossed salad that has some extra goodies thrown in: chickpeas, olives, marinated artichoke hearts. A side of spaghetti, some warm crusty garlic bread, and a glass or two of Chianti for the grown-ups, and you'll wish the kids would go to bed early.

6 chicken breasts with tenders removed (4 to 5 ounces each)
⅓ cup flour
¼ teaspoon salt
⅛ teaspoon freshly ground pepper
2 eggs
3 tablespoons plus 2 teaspoons olive oil
1 cup Italian-seasoned bread crumbs
½ cup grated Parmesan cheese
2 cups of your favorite pasta sauce
1 cup shredded mozzarella cheese

1. Chicken breasts with the tenders removed are usually quite flat. If yours aren't, pound them gently between 2 sheets of waxed paper to flatten evenly to about ⅜ inch.

2. On a plate or a sheet of waxed paper, mix the flour, salt, and pepper. In a wide, shallow soup bowl, beat the eggs with 2 teaspoons of the olive oil. On another plate, toss the bread crumbs with 3 tablespoons of the Parmesan cheese.

3. One at a time, dredge the chicken breasts in the flour; shake off any excess. Dip the breasts in the egg and then dredge in the bread crumbs to coat all over, patting them gently to help them adhere.

4. Heat the remaining 3 tablespoons olive oil in your nonstick frying pan over medium-high heat. Add the breaded chicken and cook, turning once, until golden brown on both sides and white in the center but still juicy, 2 to 3 minutes per side. Remove the cooked chicken to a platter and carefully wipe out the pan. (If it's more convenient for you, the chicken can be cooked up to a day ahead, wrapped well, and refrigerated.)

5. Shortly before serving, ladle ½ cup of the pasta sauce into the pan and swirl to cover the bottom. Arrange the cooked chicken breasts in the pan. Scatter the mozzarella cheese over the chicken. Ladle on the remaining sauce. Sprinkle the rest of the Parmesan cheese evenly over the top. Cover and bring to a simmer. The dish is ready as soon as everything is hot and the cheese is melted.

SERVES 4 TO 6

CREAMED TUNA ON TOAST

Though this quick pan supper for kids is almost as easy as tuna sandwiches, it's far more filling and comforting—a hot meal, in other words, the kind your mom always got on the table at the same time every night. Substitute buttered pasta for the toast (something curly and fun, like fusilli) and you've got an equally no-fuss cousin of tuna casserole.

2 tablespoons unsalted butter
¾ cup diced red bell pepper
⅓ cup thinly sliced scallions
2 tablespoons flour
1 cup chicken broth
1 cup milk
¼ teaspoon salt
1 can (12 ounces) chunk light tuna in water, drained
½ cup tiny frozen peas, thawed
Freshly ground black pepper
4 to 6 thick slices of toast
Shredded sharp Cheddar or grated Parmesan cheese (optional)

1. In your nonstick frying pan, melt the butter over medium heat. Add the red bell pepper, cover, and cook, stirring once or twice, until softened but still brightly colored, 3 to 4 minutes. Add the scallions and cook, stirring often, for 1 minute. Whisk in the flour and cook without browning for 2 minutes. Gradually whisk in the broth and then stir in the milk and salt. Bring to a boil, whisking until thickened and smooth. Reduce the heat to low, partially cover, and simmer, stirring often, 15 minutes.

2. Stir in the tuna, peas, and a generous grinding of pepper and continue to cook until hot, about 2 minutes. Season with additional salt and pepper to taste.

3. Set the toast on serving plates. Spoon the tuna mixture over the toast. Top with cheese, if you are using it, and serve immediately.

SERVES 4 TO 6

Pan-Barbecued Chicken Drumsticks

Quick-cooking chicken breasts are way past dry by the time they build up the proper barbecue look and flavor, which is why I turn to drumsticks when I get that BBQ craving. Drumsticks are affordable and fun to eat (definitely sticky finger food), and even with lots of turning and brushing and browning (don't rush it!), they are every bit as lusciously tender and sweetly glazed as something from the grill. The plan is always to have a few left over for lunch boxes and brown bags, but, somehow, that never happens.

1 tablespoon peanut or canola oil
8 chicken drumsticks (about 2 pounds), patted dry, at room temperature
¾ cup prepared barbecue sauce
Salt and freshly ground pepper
½ cup chicken broth

1. Warm the oil in your nonstick frying pan over medium-high heat. Add the drumsticks and cook, turning once or twice, until they are well browned, 12 to 14 minutes.

2. Brush with some of the barbecue sauce, turn, and cook for 2 minutes. Continue brushing and turning the drumsticks every 2 minutes, rearranging them to promote even cooking, until they are thoroughly glazed with sauce and tender, another 25 minutes or so. Transfer the drumsticks to a platter and season with salt and pepper to taste.

3. Add the broth to the pan and set over medium heat. Bring to a boil, stirring and scraping the bottom of the pan to dissolve the browned bits of sauce. Cook until syrupy, about 3 minutes. Pour the sauce over the drumsticks and serve hot or warm.

SERVES 4

One-Pan Mac 'n' Cheese

The inspiration for this dish comes from my young friend Charles Buckingham, who, when asked to name his favorite meal, never hesitates for a moment before answering with an aplomb worthy of the finest food critic: "mac 'n' cheese with hot dogs." Charles, this one's for you. And there's no easier version except possibly the one that comes in a box.

2½ tablespoons unsalted butter
2 tablespoons flour
1 garlic clove, crushed through a press
3 cups milk
1 teaspoon Dijon mustard
1 teaspoon paprika
½ teaspoon salt
¼ teaspoon freshly ground pepper
⅛ teaspoon grated nutmeg
2 cups elbow macaroni
3 cups shredded Cheddar cheese
2 or 3 hot dogs, sliced (optional)

1. In your nonstick frying pan, melt the butter over medium heat. Add the flour and cook, stirring, 1 minute. Add the garlic and stir for a few seconds. Pour in the milk. Add the mustard, paprika, salt, pepper, and nutmeg. Bring to a boil, whisking until slightly thickened and smooth.

2. Stir the macaroni into the cream sauce. Reduce the heat to low, cover, and cook until the macaroni is tender, about 10 minutes. Stir in the cheese.

3. Serve the mac 'n' cheese as is or for those who do, stir in the hot dog slices and simmer for 2 minutes.

SERVES 4 TO 6

Shells with Meat Sauce

In our house, the rule of thumb when cooking for the kids is the fewer seasonings the better. They love this mild meat sauce, especially when paired with pasta shells, a shape they can relate to and play with a bit, but that's a lot easier to eat than spaghetti. The onion here really helps the flavor, but be sure to cook it until meltingly soft, so the children won't know it's in there. Pass grated Parmesan or Romano cheese on the side. And garlic bread would not be amiss.

2 tablespoons olive oil
1 small onion, finely chopped
1 pound lean ground beef, such as ground round
½ can tomato paste
1 teaspoon sugar
1 can (28 ounces) Italian peeled tomatoes, coarsely chopped, juices reserved
1 teaspoon dried oregano
1 tablespoon balsamic vinegar
Salt and freshly ground pepper
¾ pound pasta shells

1. Heat the olive oil in the pan over medium-high heat. Add the onion, cover the pan, and cook for 3 minutes. Uncover, raise the heat to medium-high, and continue to cook, stirring occasionally, until the onion is very soft, about 3 minutes longer.

2. Crumble the ground beef into the pan with the onion. Cook, stirring to break up any lumps of meat, until the beef is browned, about 7 minutes.

3. Add the tomato paste and sugar to the pan. Cook, stirring constantly, 2 to 3 minutes, until the paste darkens slightly. Pour in the chopped tomatoes with their juices. Return the meat to the pan. Stir in the oregano and vinegar. Partially

cover the sauce and simmer for 45 to 60 minutes depending, upon how much time you have. Season with salt and pepper to taste.

4. In a large pot of boiling salted water, cook the pasta shells until they are tender but still firm, 10 to 12 minutes. Drain into a colander, shake once or twice, then immediately stir the shells into the meat sauce. Simmer 2 to 3 minutes and serve.

SERVES 4

Spaghetti Pie

Here's a different way to cook spaghetti, sort of a cross between an Italian torta and Asian fried noodles. Since many children don't like tomato sauce, I suggest it as an option on the side.

½ **pound thin spaghetti**
1 **tablespoon butter**
¾ **pound sweet Italian sausage, casings removed**
3½ **tablespoons olive oil**
1 **small onion, finely chopped**
½ **pound fresh mushrooms, thinly sliced**
3 **eggs**
½ **cup heavy cream**
½ **cup grated Romano cheese**
¾ **teaspoon salt**
¼ **teaspoon freshly ground pepper**
1 **cup shredded mozzarella cheese**
Marinara sauce, as accompaniment (optional)

1. In a large pot of boiling salted water, cook the spaghetti until just barely tender, 5 to 7 minutes. Drain into a colander, transfer to a large bowl, and toss with the butter to coat.

2. Crumble the sausage into your nonstick frying pan. Cook over medium heat, stirring with a wooden spoon to break up any large lumps, until the meat is lightly browned with no trace of pink, about 5 minutes. Either drain the sausage in a sieve or if there is little fat, remove with a slotted spoon. Add to the spaghetti. Wipe out the pan.

3. Add 1½ tablespoons of the olive oil to the pan and heat over medium-high heat. Add the onion and sauté for 2 minutes. Add the mushrooms and sauté until they are lightly browned, about 5 minutes. Scrape into the spaghetti.

4. In a smaller bowl, beat the eggs until blended. Whisk in the cream, Romano cheese, salt, and pepper. Pour over the spaghetti. Add the mozzarella cheese and toss to mix.

5. Heat 1 tablespoon olive oil in the pan over medium heat. Toss the spaghetti one more time and pour into the pan. Pack down with a wide spatula, cover, and cook until browned on the bottom and almost set, 4 to 5 minutes.

6. Lossen the pie with a spatula. Slide out onto a round platter or large pot lid. Pour the remaining 1 tablespoon oil into the pan and heat until hot. Invert the spaghetti pie back into the pan and cook until the second side is browned, about 3 minutes. Cut into wedges. Serve hot, either plain or with a drizzle of marinara sauce.

SERVES 4

INDEX

Almond(s)
　-honey butter, challah French toast with, 22
　pan-fried trout with lemon butter, capers, and, 107
　picadillo with raisins, olives, and, 42
　Spanish chicken sauté with olives and, 68
Apples
　pork, prunes, and, in bourbon cream sauce, 50
　skillet chicken curry with raisins, cashews, and, 86
Apricot chutney, almost-instant, pan-grilled pork chops with, 48
Arctic char, Asian-flavored, 101
Artichoke(s)
　and chicken hash, 180
　hearts with melted Fontina cheese, sautéed, 209
　skillet chicken pot pie with mixed vegetables and, 126
Arugula, spice-crusted fresh tuna on, 108
Asian-flavored Arctic char, 101
Asparagus
　with sesame oil, stir-fried, 210
　Vidalia onion, and mushroom risotto, 144
Avocado(s)
　in guacamole, 132
　and shrimp quesadillas with sizzling green salsa, 174

Bacon
　country spareribs braised with beer and, 56
　-mushroom dressing, warm spinach salad with, 194
　turkey, and Cheddar sandwiches, grilled, 171
Balsamic-Madeira reduction, Thomas's pan-fried steak with, 31

Banana rum relish, 96
　jerk chicken thighs with, Michael's, 94
Bean(s)
　black. See Black bean(s)
　and greens, garlicky, 125
　pork and, with Spanish rice, 138
　red, and rice, Southwestern, 199
　skillet salad, three-, 212
　vegetable chili with bulgur, brown rice, and, 152
Beef
　brisket, in red flannel hash, 182
　burgers with pan-grilled onions and brandy-Roquefort butter, 168
　in chili
　　Cincinnati, 149
　　five-alarm trail drive, 150
　grilled roast, and Swiss cheese sandwiches, 170
　hamburger hot dogs, 240
　meatballs, sweet 'n' sour, 238
　peppers stuffed with rice and, 154
　picadillo with raisins, olives, and almonds, 42
　pot roast, a tiny-bit-sweet pan-roasted, 40
　in skillet stuffed cabbage, 156
　Sloppy Joes, 237
　steak
　　au poivre, three-peppercorn, 32
　　with chimichurri sauce, gaucho, 38
　　flambéed in whisky, pepper-crusted pan, 34
　　with Madeira-balsamic reduction, Thomas's pan-fried, 31
　　'n' eggs with home-fried potatoes, truck stop, 16
　　pizzaiola, 36
　and vegetables in honey-tea sauce, stir-fry, 186
Beer, country spareribs braised with bacon and, 56
Bell peppers. See Pepper(s), sweet bell

Berry compote, warm, whole-grain French toast with, 24
Biscuits
    buttermilk drop, 72
    chicken 'n,' 70
Black bean(s)
    chicken chili with corn, peppers, and, 80
    quesadillas with feta cheese and pico de gallo, 178
    and rice, Mexican, 147
    salsa, quick, three-cheese quesadillas with, 172
    vegetable chili with bulgur, brown rice, and, 152
Blue cheese-brandy butter, beef burgers with pan-grilled onions and, 168
Bourbon cream sauce, pork, apples, and prunes in, 50
Braised fennel, 215
Brandy
    morels in pastry shells with cream and, 220
    -Roquefort butter, beef burgers with pan-grilled onions and, 168
Bratwurst, in choucroute, quick skillet, 52
Breakfast dishes
    challah French toast with almond-honey butter, 22
    cheesy pan soufflé, easy, 20
    eggs Florentine with smoked salmon, 14
    eggs McBoswell, 3
    eggs Santa Fe in pink salsa cream, 12
    French toast
        challah with almond-honey butter, 22
        whole-grain, with warm berry compote, 24
    frittata, Sunday morning vegetable, 6
    griddle cakes, three-grain, 26
    handkerchief egg crepes with olive filling, 18
    huevos rancheros, 10
    Mexican scramble with cheese, chiles, and salsa, 4
    midnight scrambler, 5
    omelet, Spanish potato and onion, 8
    smoked salmon scramble with cream cheese and chives, 9

steak 'n' eggs with home-fried potatoes, truck stop, 16
Brown rice, vegetable chili with bulgur, beans, and, 152
Bulgur, vegetable chili with brown rice, beans, and, 152
Burgers
    beef, with pan-grilled onions and brandy-Roquefort butter, 168
    tuna, fresh, with sesame-ginger mayonnaise, 110
    turkey, California, 167
Butter
    almond-honey, challah French toast with, 22
    brandy-Roquefort, beef burgers with pan-grilled onions and, 168
Buttermilk
    drop biscuits, 72
    flapjacks, 232
    -scallion hush puppies, 206

Cabbage, skillet stuffed, 156
Cajun tartar sauce, 103
    corn-crusted catfish with, 102
California turkey burgers, 167
Camembert, chicken breasts stuffed with spinach and, 88
Cannellini beans and greens, garlicky, 125
Caper(s)
    -mustard sauce, crab cakes with, 116
    pan-fried trout with lemon butter, almonds, and, 107
    red snapper in white wine with tomatoes and, 104
Carrot(s)
    meatball and, ragout, 158
    potato, and celery root pancakes, 204
    tropical candied, 211
Cashews, skillet chicken curry with apples, raisins, and, 86
Catfish, corn-crusted, with Cajun tartar sauce, 102
Celery root, potato, and carrot pancakes, 204
Cheddar, turkey, and bacon sandwiches, grilled, 171

Cheese
    Camembert, chicken breasts stuffed with
        spinach and, 88
    Cheddar, turkey, and bacon sandwiches,
        grilled, 171
    feta, black bean quesadillas with pico de
        gallo and, 178
    Fontina, sautéed artichoke hearts with
        melted, 209
    Mexican scramble with chiles, salsa, and, 4
    one-pan mac 'n,' 247
    Parmesan, quick chicken, 242
    pizza, white pan, 160
    provolone, skillet chicken ziti with olives
        and, 128
    quesadillas
        black bean, with feta and pico de gallo,
            178
        with quick black bean salsa, three-, 172
        shrimp and avocado, with sizzling
            green salsa, 174
    Roquefort
        -brandy butter, beef burgers with pan-
            grilled onions and, 168
        potato cakes with browned onions, 202
    Swiss cheese and grilled roast beef sand-
        wiches, 170
Cheesy pan soufflé, easy, 20
Cheesy polenta in the pan, 208
Chicken
    with African flavors, smothered, 90
    and artichoke hash, 180
    breasts
        in Madeira mushroom sauce, 78
        stuffed with spinach and Camembert,
            88
    "chicken-fried," with pan gravy, 74
    chili with corn, peppers, and black beans, 80
    curry with apples, raisins, and cashews,
        skillet, 86
    drumsticks, pan-barbecued, 246
    fajitas, 130
    faux tandoori, 66
    fried, Japanese, 65
    liver(s)
        and dirty rice, 142

        pâté with Marsala, chunky, 77
    'n' biscuits, 70
    Parmesan, quick, 242
    piccata, 84
    pot pie with artichokes and mixed vegeta-
        bles, skillet, 126
    saltimbocca, 82
    sausages and peppers, 54
    sauté with olives and almonds, Spanish, 68
    with snow peas, stir-fry jalapeño, 183
    Southern cracker–fried, 73
    stir-fry, spicy peanut, 184
    taco salad, pan-seared, 192
    thighs, jerk, with banana rum relish,
        Michael's, 94
    voodoo, 76
    wings, sticky fingers hot, 92
    ziti with olives and provolone, skillet, 128
"Chicken-fried" chicken with pan gravy, 74
Chiles, Mexican scramble with cheese, salsa,
        and, 4
Chili
    chicken, with corn, peppers, and black
        beans, 80
    Cincinnati, 149
    five-alarm trail drive, 150
Chimichurri sauce, 39
    gaucho steak with, 38
Chinese gingered eggplant in garlic sauce, 216
Chives, smoked salmon scramble with cream
        cheese and, 9
Choucroute, quick skillet, 52
Chunky chicken liver pâté with Marsala, 77
Chutney, apricot, almost-instant, pan-grilled
        pork chops with, 48
Cincinnati chili, 149
Citrus shrimp and rice, 148
Clam sauce, fresh, spaghetti with, 114
Compote, warm berry, whole-grain French
        toast with, 24
Corned beef, in red flannel hash, 182
Corn (fresh)
    chicken chili with peppers, black beans,
        and, 80
    off the cob, pan-fried, 214
Corn(meal)

-crusted catfish with Cajun tartar sauce, 102
polenta in the pan, cheesy, 208
Country spareribs braised with bacon and beer, 56
Crab cakes with mustard-caper sauce, 116
Cream
    morels in pastry shells with brandy and, 220
    pink salsa, eggs Santa Fe in, 12
    sauce, bourbon, pork, apples, and prunes in, 50
Cream cheese, smoked salmon scramble with chives and, 9
Creamed tuna on toast, 244
Creamy fettuccine with ham, mushrooms, and peas, 134
Crepes, egg, handkerchief, with olive filling, 18
Croquettes, salmon, with dill-mustard sauce, 190
Curried rice, 146

Dill-mustard sauce, salmon croquettes with, 190
Double-crusted turkey sausage pan pizzas, 162
Dr. Roland's midnight rice RX, 146
Duck fried rice, 136

Easy cheesy pan soufflé, 20
Eggplant
    in garlic sauce, Chinese gingered, 216
    in skillet ratatouille, 218
Egg(s)
    crepes with olive filling, handkerchief, 18
    Florentine with smoked salmon, 14
    frittata, Sunday morning vegetable, 6
    huevos rancheros, 10
    McBoswell, 3
    Mexican scramble with cheese, chiles, and salsa, 4
    midnight scrambler, 5
    omelet
        jelly, 236
        Spanish potato and onion, 8

Santa Fe in pink salsa cream, 12
steak 'n,' with home-fried potatoes, truck stop, 16

Fajitas, chicken, 130
Faux tandoori chicken, 66
Fennel, braised, 215
Feta cheese, black bean quesadillas with pico de gallo and, 178
Fettuccine with ham, mushrooms, and peas, creamy, 134
Fish
    catfish, corn-crusted, with Cajun tartar sauce, 102
    red snapper in white wine with tomatoes and capers, 104
    salmon. See Salmon
    trout with lemon butter, capers, and almonds, pan-fried, 107
    tuna
        burgers, fresh, with sesame-ginger mayonnaise, 110
        spice-crusted fresh, on arugula, 108
Flapjacks, buttermilk, 232
Fontina cheese, sautéed artichoke hearts with melted, 209
French toast
    challah, with almond-honey butter, 22
    whole-grain, with warm berry compote, 24
Fresh tuna burgers with sesame-ginger mayonnaise, 110
Fried rice, duck, 136
Frittata, Sunday morning vegetable, 6
Frog in the haystack, 234

Garlicky beans and greens, 125
Garlic sauce, Chinese gingered eggplant in, 216
Gaucho steak with chimichurri sauce, 38
Ginger
    pan-barbecued shrimp, triple, 118
    -sesame mayonnaise, fresh tuna burgers with, 110
Gingered eggplant in garlic sauce, Chinese, 216
Glazed ham steaks with raisin sauce, 62
Gravy, pan, "chicken-fried" chicken with, 74

Greens, garlicky beans and, 125
Green salsa, sizzling, 176
    shrimp and avocado quesadillas with, 174
Griddle cakes, three-grain, 26
Grilled roast beef and Swiss cheese sandwich-
    es, 170
Grilled turkey, bacon, and Cheddar sand-
    wiches, 171
Guacamole, 132

Ham
    creamy fettuccine with mushrooms, peas,
        and, 134
    steaks with raisin sauce, glazed, 62
Hamburger hot dogs, 240
Handkerchief egg crepes with olive filling, 18
Hash
    chicken and artichoke, 180
    red flannel, 182
Hash brown potatoes with onions and pep-
    pers, 200
Hashed sweet potatoes with orange peel and
    pecans, 222
Honey
    -almond butter, challah French toast with, 22
    tea sauce, stir-fry beef and vegetables in, 186
Hot dogs
    hamburger, 240
    in one-pan mac 'n' cheese, 247
Huevos rancheros, 10
Hush puppies, buttermilk-scallion, 206

Indian summer squash with onion and stewed
    tomatoes, 225
Italian sausages, 54

Jade spinach, 224
Jalapeño chicken with snow peas, stir-fry, 183
Jambalaya, shrimp and sausage skillet, 140
Japanese fried chicken, 65
Jelly omelet, 236
Jerk chicken thighs with banana rum relish,
    Michael's, 94
Jordan's tortilla pizza, 239

Kale, garlicky beans and, 125

Kielbasa, in quick skillet choucroute, 52

Lamb chops
    with Pernod, 58
    sautéed with sweet peppers and olives, 60
Lemon vodka sauce, veal scaloppine with, 44
Linguine, in garlicky beans and greens, 125

Mac 'n' cheese, one-pan, 247
Madeira
    -balsamic reduction, Thomas's pan-fried
        steak with, 31
    mushroom sauce, chicken breasts in, 78
Marsala, chunky chicken liver pâté with, 77
Mayonnaise, sesame-ginger, fresh tuna burg-
    ers with, 110
Meatball(s)
    and carrot ragout, 158
    sweet 'n' sour, 238
Meat sauce, shells with, 248
Mexican black beans and rice, 147
Mexican scramble with cheese, chiles, and
    salsa, 4
Midnight scrambler, 5
Monterey Jack cheese, in Mexican scramble
    with cheese, chiles, and salsa, 4
Morels in pastry shells with brandy and
    cream, 220
Mozzarella cheese
    in Jordan's tortilla pizza, 239
    in spaghetti pie, 250
Mushroom(s)
    asparagus, and Vidalia onion risotto, 144
    -bacon dressing, warm spinach salad with,
        194
    creamy fettuccine with ham, peas, and,
        134
    morels in pastry shells with brandy and
        cream, 220
    sauce, Madeira, chicken breasts in, 78
    turkey and, paprikash, 97
Mussels, pan-steamed, 120
Mustard
    -caper sauce, crab cakes with, 116
    -glazed salmon steaks, 106
    sauce, dill-, salmon croquettes with, 190

Olive(s)
    filling, handkerchief egg crepes with, 18
    lamb chops sautéed with sweet peppers
        and, 60
    picadillo with raisins, almonds, and, 42
    skillet chicken ziti with provolone and,
        128
    Spanish chicken sauté with almonds and,
        68
Omelet
    jelly, 236
    Spanish potato and onion, 8
One-pan mac 'n' cheese, 247
Onion(s)
    beef burgers with pan-grilled, and brandy-
        Roquefort butter, 168
    hash brown potatoes with peppers and,
        200
    Indian summer squash with stewed toma-
        toes and, 225
    and potato omelet, Spanish, 8
    Roquefort potato cakes with browned, 202
    Vidalia, asparagus, and mushroom risotto,
        144
Orange
    -flavor pork with vegetables, 188
    peel and pecans, hashed sweet potatoes
        with, 222
Orzo pilaf, salmon-, 133
Oyster pan roast, 119

Pan-barbecued chicken drumsticks, 246
Pancakes, potato, carrot, and celery root, 204
Pan-fried corn off the cob, 214
Pan-fried trout with lemon butter, capers, and
    almonds, 107
Pan gravy, "chicken-fried" chicken with, 74
Pan-grilled pork chops with almost-instant
    apricot chutney, 48
Pan-seared chicken taco salad, 192
Pan-steamed mussels, 120
Parmesan, quick chicken, 242
Pasta
    fettuccine with ham, mushrooms, and
        peas, creamy, 134
    linguine, in garlicky beans and greens, 125

    mac 'n' cheese, one-pan, 247
    salmon-orzo pilaf, 133
    shells with meat sauce, 248
    spaghetti pie, 250
    spaghetti with fresh clam sauce, 114
    ziti with olives and provolone, skillet
        chicken, 128
Pâté, chunky chicken liver, with Marsala, 77
Peanut butter, in voodoo chicken, 76
Peanut chicken stir-fry, spicy, 184
Peas, creamy fettuccine with ham, mush-
    rooms, and, 134
Pecans, hashed sweet potatoes with orange
    peel and, 222
Pepper(corns)
    -crusted pan steak flambéed in whisky, 34
    steak au poivre, three-, 32
Pepper(s), sweet bell
    chicken chili with corn, black beans, and,
        80
    hash brown potatoes with onions and, 200
    lamb chops sautéed with olives and, 60
    red, in skillet ratatouille, 218
    sausages and, 54
    stuffed with beef and rice, 154
Pernod, lamb chops with, 58
Picadillo with raisins, olives, and almonds, 42
Pico de gallo, black bean quesadillas with feta
    cheese and, 178
Pie, spaghetti, 250
Pilaf, salmon-orzo, 133
Pinto beans, vegetable chili with bulgur,
    brown rice, and, 152
Pizza(s)
    pan
        turkey sausage, double-crusted, 162
        white, 160
    tortilla, Jordan's, 239
Polenta in the pan, cheesy, 208
Pork
    apples, and prunes in bourbon cream
        sauce, 50
    and beans with Spanish rice, 138
    in chili, five-alarm trail drive, 150
    chops with almost-instant apricot chutney,
        pan-grilled, 48

country ribs, in quick skillet choucroute, 52

country spareribs braised with bacon and beer, 56

with vegetables, orange-flavor, 188

Potato(es)

cakes with browned onions, Roquefort, 202

carrot, and celery root pancakes, 204

hash brown, with onions and peppers, 200

home-fried, truck stop steak 'n' eggs with, 16

and onion omelet, Spanish, 8

Pot roast, a tiny-bit-sweet pan-roasted, 40

Prosciutto, in eggs McBoswell, 3

Provolone, skillet chicken ziti with olives and, 128

Prunes, pork, apples, and, in bourbon cream sauce, 50

Quesadillas

black bean, with feta cheese and pico de gallo, 178

with quick black bean salsa, three-cheese, 172

shrimp and avocado, with sizzling green salsa, 174

Quick chicken Parmesan, 242

Quick skillet choucroute, 52

Ragout, meatball and carrot, 158

Raisin(s)

picadillo with olives, almonds, and, 42

sauce, glazed ham steaks with, 62

skillet chicken curry with apples, cashews, and, 86

Ratatouille, skillet, 218

Red beans and rice, Southwestern, 199

Red flannel hash, 182

Red snapper, in white wine with tomatoes and capers, 104

Refried beans, in huevos rancheros, 10

Relish, banana rum, 96

jerk chicken thighs with, Michael's, 94

Rice

black beans and, Mexican, 147

brown, vegetable chili with bulgur, beans, and, 152

chicken livers and dirty, 142

citrus shrimp and, 148

curried, 146

Dr. Roland's midnight rice RX, 146

duck fried, 136

peppers stuffed with beef and, 154

red beans and, Southwestern, 199

Spanish, pork and beans with, 138

Risotto, asparagus, Vidalia onion, and mushroom, 144

Roast beef and Swiss cheese sandwiches, grilled, 170

Roquefort

-brandy butter, beef burgers with pan-grilled onions and, 168

potato cakes with browned onions, 202

Rosemary veal chops with quick pan sauce, 46

Salad

chicken taco, pan-seared, 192

spinach, warm, with mushroom-bacon dressing, 194

three-bean skillet, 212

Salmon

croquettes with dill-mustard sauce, 190

-orzo pilaf, 133

smoked

eggs Florentine with, 14

scramble with cream cheese and chives, 9

steaks, mustard-glazed, 106

Salsa

black bean, quick, three-cheese quesadillas with, 172

cream, pink, eggs Santa Fe in, 12

Mexican scramble with cheese, chiles, and, 4

sizzling green, 176

shrimp and avocado quesadillas with, 174

Saltimbocca chicken, 82

Sandwiches

grilled roast beef and Swiss cheese, 170

grilled turkey, bacon, and Cheddar, 171

Sauce
chimichurri, 39
gaucho steak with, 38
clam, fresh, spaghetti with, 114
cream, bourbon, pork, apples, and prunes
in, 50
dill-mustard, salmon croquettes with, 190
garlic, Chinese gingered eggplant in, 216
honey-tea, stir-fry beef and vegetables in, 186
Madeira mushroom, chicken breasts in, 78
meat, shells with, 248
mustard-caper, crab cakes with, 116
raisin, glazed ham steaks with, 62
tartar, Cajun, 103
corn-crusted catfish with, 102
tomato
in steak pizzaiola, 36
too many tomatoes and sweet sausage,
226
vodka, lemon, veal scaloppine with, 44
Sauerkraut, in choucroute, quick skillet, 52
Sausage(s)
in frog in the haystack, 234
and peppers, 54
shrimp and, skillet jambalaya, 140
sweet Italian
in spaghetti pie, 250
tomato sauce, too many tomatoes and,
226
turkey, pan pizzas, double-crusted, 162
Sautéed artichoke hearts with melted Fontina
cheese, 209
Scallion, buttermilk-, hush puppies, 206
Sesame-ginger mayonnaise, fresh tuna burgers
with, 110
Sesame oil, stir-fried asparagus with, 210
Shells with meat sauce, 248
Shrimp
au poivre, 112
and avocado quesadillas with sizzling
green salsa, 174
and rice, citrus, 148
and sausage skillet jambalaya, 140
triple ginger pan-barbecued, 118
Sizzling green salsa, 176
shrimp and avocado quesadillas with, 174

Skillet chicken curry with apples, raisins, and
cashews, 86
Skillet chicken pot pie with artichokes and
mixed vegetables, 126
Skillet chicken ziti with olives and provolone,
128
Skillet ratatouille, 218
Skillet stuffed cabbage, 156
Sloppy Joes, 237
Smoked salmon
eggs Florentine with, 14
scramble with cream cheese and chives, 9
Smothered chicken with African flavors, 90
Snow peas, stir-fry jalapeño chicken with, 183
Soufflé, easy cheesy pan, 20
Southern cracker–fried chicken, 73
Southwestern red beans and rice, 199
Spaghetti
with fresh clam sauce, 114
pie, 250
Spanish chicken sauté with olives and
almonds, 68
Spanish potato and onion omelet, 8
Spareribs, country, braised with bacon and
beer, 56
Spice-crusted fresh tuna on arugula, 108
Spicy peanut chicken stir-fry, 184
Spinach
chicken breasts stuffed with Camembert
and, 88
in eggs Florentine with smoked salmon, 14
jade, 224
salad with mushroom-bacon dressing,
warm, 194
Squash, summer, with onion and stewed
tomatoes, Indian, 225
Sticky fingers hot wings, 92
Stir-fried asparagus with sesame oil, 210
Stir-fry
beef and vegetables in honey-tea sauce, 186
jalapeño chicken with snow peas, 183
spicy peanut chicken, 184
Summer squash with onion and stewed tomatoes, Indian, 225
Sunday morning vegetable frittata, 6
Sweet 'n' sour meatballs, 238

Sweet potatoes with orange peel and pecans, hashed, 222
Swiss cheese and grilled roast beef sandwiches, 170

Taco salad, pan-seared chicken, 192
Tandoori chicken, faux, 66
Tartar sauce, Cajun, 103
   corn-crusted catfish with, 102
Thomas's pan-fried steak with Madeira-balsamic reduction, 31
Three-bean skillet salad, 212
Three-cheese quesadillas with quick black bean salsa, 172
Three-grain griddle cakes, 26
Three-peppercorn steak au poivre, 32
Tiny-bit-sweet pan-roasted pot roast, a, 40
Tomato(es)
   red snapper in white wine with capers and, 104
   sauce
      in steak pizzaiola, 36
      too many tomatoes and sweet sausage, 226
   in skillet ratatouille, 218
   stewed, in midnight scrambler, 5
   stewed, Indian summer squash with onion and, 225
Too many tomatoes and sweet sausage tomato sauce, 226
Tortilla(s)
   chips, in Mexican scramble with cheese, chiles, and salsa, 4
   pizza, Jordan's, 239
   warm corn, 231
Triple ginger pan-barbecued shrimp, 118
Tropical candied carrots, 211
Trout with lemon butter, capers, and almonds, pan-fried, 107
Truck stop steak 'n' eggs with home-fried potatoes, 16
Tuna
   burgers, fresh, with sesame-ginger mayonnaise, 110
   spice-crusted fresh, on arugula, 108
   on toast, creamed, 244

Turkey
   bacon, and Cheddar sandwiches, grilled, 171
   burgers, California, 167
   and mushroom paprikash, 97
   sausage pan pizzas, double-crusted, 162

Veal
   chops with quick pan sauce, rosemary, 46
   scaloppine with lemon vodka sauce, 44
Vegetable(s)
   chili with bulgur, brown rice, and beans, 152
   frittata, Sunday morning, 6
   orange-flavor pork with, 188
   skillet chicken pot pie with artichokes and mixed, 126
   stir-fry beef and, in honey-tea sauce, 186
Vodka sauce, lemon, veal scaloppine with, 44
Voodoo chicken, 76

Warm corn tortillas, 231
Warm spinach salad with mushroom-bacon dressing, 194
Whisky, pepper-crusted pan steak flambéed in, 34
White beans and greens, garlicky, 125
White pan pizza, 160
White wine, red snapper in, with tomatoes and capers, 104
Whole-grain French toast with warm berry compote, 24

Ziti, skillet chicken, with olives and provolone, 128
Zucchini, in skillet ratatouille, 218